ALL OUT WAR

ALL OUT WAR

WAR

THE PLOT TO DESTROY TRUMP

EDWARD KLEIN

REGNERY
PUBLISHING

A Division of Salem Media Group

Regnery® is a registered trademark of Salem Communications Holding Corporation

Cataloging-in-Publication data on file with the Library of Congress

ISBN 978-1-62157-698-3

Published in the United States by
Regnery Publishing
A Division of Salem Media Group
300 New Jersey Ave NW
Washington, DC 20001
www.Regnery.com

Manufactured in the United States of America

10 9 8 7 6 5 4 3 2 1

Some passages in this book originally appeared in *Ed Klein Confidential*, the author's weekly blog.

Books are available in quantity for promotional or premium use. For information on discounts and terms, please visit our website: www. Regnery.com.

ALSO BY EDWARD KLEIN

NONFICTION

All Too Human:
The Love Story of Jack and Jackie Kennedy

Just Jackie:
Her Private Years

The Kennedy Curse:
Why Tragedy Has Haunted America's First Family for 150 Years

Farewell, Jackie: A Portrait of Her Final Days

The Truth about Hillary:
What She Knew, When She Knew It,
and How Far She'll Go to Become President

Katie:
The Real Story

Ted Kennedy:
The Dream That Never Died

The Amateur:
Barack Obama in the White House

Blood Feud:
The Clintons vs. the Obamas

Unlikeable:
The Problem with Hillary

Guilty as Sin

NOVELS

If Israel Lost the War
(With Robert Littell and Richard Z. Chesnoff)

The Parachutists

The Obama Identity
(With John LeBoutillier)

ANTHOLOGIES

About Men
(With Don Erickson)

For Dan Strone

CONTENTS

PART THREE: FIRST HUNDRED DAYS

PART FOUR: SIEGE

I'm very much alive
I still got the jive to survive with the heroes and villains.

—The Beach Boys, "Heroes and Villains"

INTRODUCTION

THE CORNERSTONE OF AMERICAN DEMOCRACY

I n America, you are entitled to your own opinion, but you are not entitled to overthrow the democratically elected president of the United States and inflict irreparable damage on our country.

That, however, is what Donald Trump's enemies on the Left and Right are doing. Through a variety of underhanded tactics—lies, leaks, obstruction, and violence—they are waging an all-out war to delegitimize President Trump and drive him from office before he can drain the swamp and take away their power.

Who are these determined and ruthless villains?

You've heard of many of them—Elizabeth Warren, Al Franken, George Soros. You've seen their names on Facebook and Twitter and heard them on TV—Jake Tapper, Don Lemon, Rachel Maddow. Others may be unfamiliar to you—Neera Tanden, Tom Steyer, Anna Galland. Still others are nameless—members of the permanent government, the so-called Deep State.

What all the villains have in common is their refusal to accept Donald Trump as their president. They live in an alternate universe of *if-onlies*: Hillary Clinton would have won the election *if only* the Russians hadn't meddled in the election, *if only* FBI Director James Comey hadn't reopened the investigation of Hillary's emails shortly before Election Day, *if only* Bernie Sanders hadn't damaged Hillary in the primaries, *if only* male voters hadn't been women-haters, *if only* the Democratic National Committee had gotten its act together, *if only* there weren't so many "deplorables" in America, *if only*...

"Right up until election night," writes the *Washington Examiner*'s Michael Barone, "[the Democrats] believed that the future was forever theirs. Between 9:00 and 10:00 p.m. on Election Night, it became clear that this was...the god that failed."

The villains have incited so much anti-Trump hysteria that the phenomenon has acquired a name. It's called Trump Derangement Syndrome, and its symptoms range from the farcical to the terrifying:

- After the election, liberal women in Washington, DC, swarmed the Georgetown Salon & Spa and demanded that their hairdressers chop off their locks or change their hair color as a way to protest the outcome
- *Cosmopolitan* magazine ran a headline: "I Haven't Had Sex in Weeks. I Blame Donald Trump"
- ABC's Martha Raddatz, who hosted a presidential debate, teared up on camera when she learned that Trump won the presidency
- Democrats, including California Congresswoman Maxine Waters, talked openly about impeaching Trump even before he took office
- Reza Aslan, the host of CNN's "Believer," tweeted that Trump was "a piece of shit" who is "a stain on the presidency"
- A Bernie Sanders zealot opened fire on congressional Republicans practicing for a baseball game, seriously wounding House Whip Steve Scalise and injuring four others

The villains are prepared to overthrow the Trump presidency even if it undermines the cornerstone of American democracy—the peaceful transfer of power.

For 221 years—ever since John Adams defeated Thomas Jefferson in the election of 1796—the losing party has conceded defeat and moved on. That happened even after elections that were won by the squeakiest of margins—Kennedy vs. Nixon, Carter vs. Ford, Bush vs. Gore. This sacred tradition is being called into question for the first time in our history.

The villains are winning battle after battle against President Trump. He and his aides are the target of several congressional investigations, illegal leaks by the Deep State, daily lashings by the media, and Special Counsel Robert Mueller, who is examining charges of obstruction of justice.

"Much of Washington clearly views Mr. Mueller as their agent to rid the country of a President they despise," writes the *Wall Street Journal*. "Every political and social incentive in that city will press Mr. Mueller to oblige. But you cannot topple a duly elected President based merely on innuendo or partisan distaste without doing great harm to democracy."

There are villains on both sides of the political divide. Those on the Left want to impeach Trump. Those on the Right—people in his own party who are disloyal to Trump—want to invoke the Twenty-Fifth Amendment to the Constitution, under which the cabinet would remove the president and replace him with Vice President Mike Pence.

Either course of action would amount to a coup d'état.

I wrote this book because the time is getting short to stop the villains from overthrowing our president. If you want to join the effort to prevent the villains from destroying our democracy, then this book—more than a year in the making and based on never-before-published information—is your essential guide.

PROLOGUE

THE OBAMA WHISPERER

CHRISTMASTIME, 2016

"I was having dinner in the White House when Susan Rice came in and gave me a dirty look. Susan is ferociously competitive, and it galled her that I'd been invited to have dinner with the Obamas while she'd been asked for coffee and dessert."

The speaker was a close friend of the president's consigliere Valerie Jarrett. She had invited him to join Barack and Michelle Obama in the Family Dining Room, and he was recalling the moment toward the end of the evening when Susan Rice, the national security adviser, joined the group. Though she arrived as the dinner plates were being cleared away, Rice was actually the prime focus of the evening. She was there to unveil a plan to sabotage President-elect Donald Trump even before he had a chance to assume office.

"Susan is an abrasive character," Jarrett's friend said, "but she's been with Barack from the beginning of his political rise, and he trusted her.

1

Michelle had a completely different take on Susan. She thought Susan was careless and reckless, a lousy advocate for the president, and she blamed Susan for a lot of things, including the clumsy way she handled Benghazi and the Bowe Bergdahl prisoner exchange, which made the president look bad.[1]

"Michelle didn't want to have to sit through an entire dinner with Susan," he continued, "so she asked Valerie to invite her for coffee and dessert. Michelle wanted to make sure Barack understood the risk he was running if he went along with Susan's scheme to cripple Trump."

Obama knew what Rice was doing. He knew she had asked the National Security Agency to "unmask," or disclose, the names of several Trump campaign associates who were mentioned or whose conversations were captured in intelligence intercepts of Russian officials.

He knew Rice wanted him to sign orders permitting the National Security Agency to lower the secrecy classification of these intercepts and disseminate the unmasked names to sixteen other intelligence agencies, allowing hundreds of people throughout the government to have access to the names of Trump's campaign aides appearing in the intercepts.

And he knew Rice wanted to encourage leaks to the *Washington Post* and the *New York Times* accusing Trump and his campaign of colluding with Russian President Vladimir Putin in the American presidential election.

What he didn't know was what Valerie Jarrett, whose powerful hold over the president had earned her the nickname The Obama Whisperer, thought of this political intrigue. Her opinion invariably guided his own, and this time around the stakes couldn't have been higher.

If Rice's plot succeeded—that is, if it could be proved that Trump had colluded with Putin during the campaign or, later, if it could be proved that he had tried to prevent an investigation into such collusion—Trump would likely face charges of impeachment.

On the other hand, if Rice's plot failed—that is, if Trump could prove that Obama had abused his power and employed the intelligence community as a political weapon against him—Obama's reputation would lie in ruins.

■ ■ ■

"Dinner in the Family Quarters always started promptly at 6:30, because Michelle wanted Malia and Sasha to learn the virtue of being on time," Valerie Jarrett's friend explained. "That night, as usual, the president came directly from the Oval Office and was still in his suit and tie.

"The dining room—the entire White House—was filled with the pleasant odor of Christmas trees," he went on, "but there wasn't any holiday spirit. You could feel the sense of gloom around the table. Ever since Trump's victory, he had been bragging about how he was going to destroy everything the Obamas had worked for for eight years—Obamacare, the Iran nuclear deal, the Trans-Pacific Partnership, the Paris climate agreement, you name it.

"Michelle was in terrible shape; she complained about migraine headaches. The president was suffering from insomnia; he had been prescribed Ambien to help him get some sleep. The Obamas were about to leave for their Christmas vacation in Hawaii, and the dinner was the president's last chance to review Rice's plan to stop Trump's one-man wrecking machine."

It wasn't until well after seven o'clock that Susan Rice showed up. She was a diminutive woman—just five foot three inches tall—with an outsized personality and a reputation for having the foulest mouth in the Obama administration. Examples of her obscenity-laden outbursts were the stuff of Washington legend. For instance, after a meeting with a negotiator for the Palestinian Authority, she exploded: "You fucking Palestinians can never see the fucking big picture." Another time, she called a high-ranking German official a "motherfucker."

"Susan was uncharacteristically nervous when she sat down at the table," Valerie Jarrett's friend said. "She had to struggle to raise a smile. She didn't look around the room, just at the notes she had in her hand.

"She said that the names of several of Trump's aides appeared in the intelligence summaries that she and Ben Rhodes [her deputy] had been examining, and she began to read off some of their names, including Michael Flynn [Trump's choice for national security adviser]. But Barack waved his hand to stop her, and Michelle broke in and said, 'We get it, we get it.'

"Michelle then asked, 'The use of these intelligence summaries about the Trump people—is this a political thing? Are you talking about using the intelligence to sandbag Trump? Because that's what it sure sounds like.'

"Susan said, and I'm paraphrasing: 'No, no, this is about national security. We've established that the Russians were behind the hacking of the DNC [Democratic National Committee] and [John] Podesta [Hillary Clinton's campaign manager]. Flynn wasn't the only one of Trump's people who had calls and meetings with [Russian ambassador Sergey] Kislyak and other Russian officials. And there are intercepts by our allies of Russian officials in the Kremlin discussing their contacts with Trump's people.'

"Susan then recommended that the president issue an order lowering the security classification level of the documents and spread them around the intelligence community. This would allow the intelligence to be uploaded to Intellipedia, an online wiki system used by intelligence analysts to share information. She said she was afraid that once Trump got into the White House, the evidence of collusion would be covered up or destroyed.

"Michelle interrupted again and asked: 'Is that *really* why you want to lower the security clearance? To preserve it, not to get Trump?'

"Susan nodded her head.

"Michelle looked exasperated. Then she said, 'And wouldn't that kind of wide distribution increase the likelihood of leaks?'

"Susan nodded her head again.

"'Is that your objective?' Michelle asked. 'Leaks against Trump?'

"Susan didn't answer.

"'Leaks like that can come back to bite us in the ass,' Michelle said.

"At this point, Barack got up and walked across the room. He often paced a room when he was weighing a difficult decision. He went over to a waiter standing near the kitchen and asked him for a brandy. Then he returned to the table. I thought for a second he was going to say something about the abuse of presidential power, maybe about the risk of leaking classified material, which is illegal and can send you to prison, but he didn't say anything.

"By now, Susan had fallen silent, too. There was an uncomfortable moment during which nobody said a word.

"I looked over at the president. In his position, nothing was ever black and white. Most of the time he had to choose between the lesser of two evils. This was an example of such a dilemma. It was clearly unethical to use illegal leaks to sabotage Trump. But Barack could argue that it was his patriotic to duty to draw attention to the possibility that the Trump campaign had conspired with the Russians to influence the outcome of an American election.

"Then Valerie piped up. 'Well,' she said, '[FBI Director James] Comey thinks Susan's onto something. He's investigating whether the Trump campaign cooperated with the Russians. There must be something there.'

"Valerie has a sixth sense how to handle Barack and Michelle. She understood Michelle's reservations and her desire to protect her husband, and she wanted to give Michelle a chance to vent. But Valerie left no doubt that she was in favor of Barack going along with Susan's scheme.

"Now it was clear that Susan could move ahead with her plan unless the president explicitly ordered her not to. But Barack sat there and said nothing. His silence was tantamount to giving Susan approval to go after Trump.

"At that point, Valerie thanked Susan for coming—dismissing her from the table. Susan collected her notes and left. I noticed she hadn't touched her coffee or key lime pie."

PART ONE

CAMPAIGN

1

UNPRESIDENTIAL

I f we are going to be honest with ourselves in assigning blame for the unhinged assault on Donald Trump, we must start with the villainy of Never-Trump Republicans who opposed Trump's nomination, disapproved of his campaign and, in many cases, still resist his presidency.

This includes a vast array of prominent party figures, establishment conservatives, and moderates:

- Two former presidents (both Bushes)
- Five GOP presidential primary candidates
- Twenty-two former cabinet-level officials
- Twenty current and former governors
- Seventeen current and former U.S. senators
- Sixty-two current and former members of the House of Representatives

- Twenty-eight former State Department officials
- Sixteen former Defense Department officials
- Twenty-five former national security officials
- Fifty-seven conservative academics, commentators, and journalists

The editors of *National Review*, the granddaddy of conservative publications, devoted an entire issue at the beginning of 2016 headlined "Against Trump."

"We sympathize with many of the complaints of Trump supporters about the GOP, but that doesn't make the mogul any less flawed a vessel for them," the editors of the magazine wrote. "Some conservatives have made it their business to make excuses for Trump and duly get pats on the head from him. Count us out. Donald Trump is a menace to American conservatism who would take the work of generations and trample it underfoot in behalf of a populism as heedless and crude as the Donald himself."

The *Weekly Standard*, the voice of the neoconservative wing of the Republican Party, was equally harsh in its assessment of Trump.

"Arguably, the single biggest story of the 2016 presidential contest has been how Trump's candidacy has divided the Republican Party," wrote Stephen F. Hayes, the magazine's editor-in-chief. Hayes accused Trump of "casual dishonesty" and alleged that such dishonesty was "a feature of his campaign. And it's one of the many reasons so many Republicans and conservatives oppose Trump and will never support his candidacy. I'm one of them."

No one attacked Trump more fiercely than two Republican politicians—Jeff Flake, the Arizona senator, who released a book criticizing the president, and Mitt Romney, the party's 2012 presidential candidate, who, ironically, had asked for and received Trump's endorsement in 2012. Romney delivered a jeremiad against Trump at the University of Utah during the height of the 2016 GOP primary campaign.

"I am far from the first to conclude that Donald Trump lacks the temperament to be president," Romney said. "After all, this is an individual who mocked a disabled reporter, who attributed a reporter's questions to her menstrual cycle, who mocked a brilliant rival who happened to be a woman due to her appearance, who bragged about his marital affairs, and who laces his public speeches with vulgarity.

"Here's what I know," Romney concluded. "Donald Trump is a phony, a fraud. His promises are as worthless as a degree from Trump University. He's playing the American public for suckers: He gets a free ride to the White House and all we get is a lousy [Make America Great Again] hat."

John Weaver, the chief strategist for the 2016 presidential campaign of Ohio's Republican governor John Kasich, was eager for Kasich to challenge Trump for the nomination in 2020. "Gangrene has entered into the body, and either you join in the effort to cut it out—to kill it—or you acquiesce to it," he said. "We can't stand by and allow racists, neo-Nazis, white supremacists, anti-Semites—whatever you want to call them—free rein in the public discourse. They cannot be normalized."

And Kasich, who refused to support Trump in the general election, and never missed a chance to take a shot at Trump, dropped hints that he was prepared to launch a primary challenge to the incumbent president in 2020.

■　■　■

Many people—I among them—scratch their heads in puzzlement over these attacks from the Right. What exactly do conservative and Republican naysayers have against Trump?

He is in favor of repealing and replacing Obamacare.

So are they.

He is in favor of cutting taxes and reforming the tax code.

So are they.

He is in favor of removing excessive regulations on business.

So are they.

He is in favor of securing America's borders.

So are they.

He is in favor of the Keystone XL Pipeline.

So are they.

He is in favor of repairing America's crumbling infrastructure.

So are they.

He is in favor of appointing "originalists" to the Supreme Court.

So are they.

He is in favor of school choice.

So are they.

He is pro-life.

So are they.

He is in favor of religious freedom and free speech.

So are they.

He is in favor of the right to bear arms.

So are they.

He is in favor of law enforcement and cracking down on crime.

So are they.

Yet his critics on the Right argue that Trump isn't a true conservative. They have an assortment of complaints.

They point out that when he was a businessman Trump contributed to both parties and that Trump himself changed his party registration. But so did Ronald Reagan.

They charge that Trump has no political experience; that he didn't pay his dues by working his way up within the ranks of the Republican Party. This is true, but Trump voters hold that to his credit. They resent a Republican Party that seems big on talk and short on action; they believe that a businessman, focused on results, may do better.

Some Never-Trumpers say they distrust him because on important issues like health care and abortion, he changed his opinions—even if he changed them in a more conservative way; and even if, as any honest reader could attest, Trump's three political books since 2000 were remarkably consistent and largely conservative.

Many other Never-Trumpers assert that Trump's stance on trade and foreign policy doesn't fit a conservative free trade and interventionist orthodoxy. But few conservatives have ever been free trade absolutists—Reagan wasn't—and outside of the neoconservative clique, internationalism has never been a Republican article of faith. In fact, Trump's assertion of a realist foreign policy, guided by America's national interest, however bluntly expressed, is very much in the mold of traditional American conservatism.

On closer inspection, it seems to me that the major objection to Trump among establishment conservatives and Republicans has little to do with his stands on economic, domestic, or foreign policy. It is almost entirely about his manner, his style, and his appearance. I have heard many of Trump's right-wing critics complain about the way he dresses ("he doesn't button his jacket"), his hair ("a comb over"), his tan ("fake"), his manner of speech ("crude"), and his attacks on his opponents ("way over the top").

Trump offends their sensibility.

These conservatives and Republicans are put off by Trump's "vulgarity." They feel that their taste and manners are superior to his. They don't want to sound like snobs, so they settle on a code word to explain their anti-Trump sentiment: *presidential.*

Donald Trump isn't presidential.

There is truth to that charge. He *isn't* presidential.

According to my sources in the Trump campaign, after Mitt Romney's vicious attack, a fierce debate broke out among Trump's family, friends, and campaign advisers over what to do about Trump's lack of self-control and unpresidential behavior. Heated disagreement inside the campaign intensified when the primary race tightened, and a group of mega-rich Republican donors started pouring millions of dollars into anti-Trump commercials in Florida, which held its crucial primary on March 15.

Members of the Republican establishment—a good old boy network of donors, elected officials, local and state party officials, pollsters, advisers, and conservative pooh-bahs who thought they should run the show—were desperate to prevent Trump from winning the 1,237 delegates needed to claim the GOP nomination. (The prize in Florida was ninety-nine delegates.) They wanted to throw the nomination onto the floor of a contested convention in July, where they could pick a candidate more acceptable to them.

Some of Trump's advisers urged him to stop acting like an Alpha dog, drop the narcissistic me-me-me, refrain from counterattacking his opponents, and focus more on substance and policy. Others urged him to reach into his pockets and invest millions of his own money in TV commercials to answer the establishment's negative ads.

But Trump ignored their advice.

"Why should I change?" Trump told me during one of several phone conversations we had at the time. "I'm going to continue with the strategy that got me where I am."

One of his advisers added: "He's going to rely on Twitter, Facebook, and large campaign rallies, and he has no intention of pouring millions into TV commercials. As for becoming more presidential, let me quote Donald and you'll get the gist. He says and I quote, 'I don't want to be a jerk. I have to do what I have to do. If people attack me, I'm going to attack them even harder and they'll live to regret it.'"

With Donald Trump, what you see is what you get.

And some 62,979,636 voters liked what they saw.

2

PUTIN'S PAYBACK

One of the great villains in this story is Vladimir Vladimirovich Putin. But in order to understand Putin's motives we must go back several years, to May 7, 2012, and pick up the Putin story as he headed to his third inauguration as president of Russia.

Flanked by motorcycle outriders, a black Mercedes carried Putin through the empty streets of Moscow. There wasn't a soul to cheer him on. The *politsiya* had blocked off the route of his motorcade as a precaution against protests by Muscovites who opposed Putin's government of thieves. As one foreign journalist noted, Putin was forced to make the journey to the Kremlin "silently and alone."

Putin's Mercedes sped through the gates of the Spasskaya Tower to the steps of the Grand Kremlin Palace. With his long swinging macho strides, he made his way along a red carpet into the ornate Andreyevsky Hall, where he was greeted by 3,000 guests, including many foreigners. Putin looked pleased until he noticed the American representative, a junior official who had been sent to Moscow for the occasion by Secretary of State Hillary Clinton.

"Putin was furious," said a diplomat who recalled the event in an interview for this book. "Japan sent its prime minister, China its president, and Putin took it as a personal insult that Hillary had sent such an insignificant person to his inauguration. He believed that Hillary had gone out of her way to disrespect him by sending a junior Foreign Service officer, who also happened to be gay. Hillary knew that Putin hated and persecuted homosexuals.

"I'm amused when people say that Putin interfered in the American presidential election because he and Donald Trump were close and liked each other," the diplomat continued. "They didn't even know each other. They'd never met. Sure, Putin probably thought he could get along with a businessman like Trump. But that wasn't his primary motivation. Putin hated Hillary far more than he liked Trump."

■ ■ ■

Putin's bitter feelings could be traced back to 2008, when Hillary was running against Barack Obama for the Democratic Party's presidential nomination and was trying to convince voters that a woman had the strength to be commander in chief. She mocked Obama for his inexperience and naïveté in foreign affairs, and compared him to George W. Bush, who famously remarked that he had looked into Vladimir Putin's eyes and "was able to get a sense of his soul."

"I could have told him," Hillary said, "[Putin] was a KGB agent. By definition he doesn't have a soul."

That was Putin's first taste of what it would be like to deal with Hillary Clinton. From then on, in conversations with his Kremlin cronies, he ridiculed Hillary as "a lady with balls."

After Barack Obama won the election and appointed Hillary secretary of state, she made a trip to Russia. Hillary's visit was supposed to be part of a much ballyhooed "reset" of American-Russian relations to a more cordial level than had existed during the administration of George W. Bush. But things did not go well. Putin invited her to his dacha outside Moscow and showed off his trophy room, which was filled with the mounted heads of animals he had shot. He did everything he could to intimidate her, short of taking off his shirt and flexing his well-photographed pecs.

Later, during a photo op outside the dacha, Putin berated Hillary in front of the assembled journalists. Among other things, he accused her of trying to undermine the Russian economy—and prevent Russia's reemergence as a geopolitical counterbalance to America—by purposely erecting barriers to trade.

The tipping point in their relationship came in 2011, when Hillary criticized Russia's fraudulent parliamentary elections. As massive demonstrations broke out across Russia, Hillary declared that the Russian people "deserve to have their voices heard and their votes counted, and that means they deserve fair, free transparent elections and leaders who are accountable to them."

Putin interpreted Hillary's words as an effort by the United States to encourage regime change in Russia.

"At a crisis meeting with his advisers," wrote Simon Shuster, a *Time* magazine correspondent, "the Russian leader chose to lay the blame [for the demonstrations] on one meddling foreign diplomat: U.S. Secretary of State Hillary Clinton."

"She set the tone for certain actors inside the country; she gave the signal," Putin fumed. "She said [the elections] were dishonest and unfair. [The protestors] heard this signal and, with the support of the U.S. State Department, started actively doing their work."

Putin's attack on Hillary only seemed to whet her appetite for combat. After Putin annexed Crimea and invaded eastern Ukraine, claiming he was defending the rights of ethnic Russians, Hillary pounced on him.

"Now if this sounds familiar," Hillary said, "it's what Hitler did back in the '30s.... Hitler kept saying: 'They're not being treated right. I must go and protect my people.' And that's what's gotten everybody so nervous."

Twenty million Russians died at the hands of Hitler's armies in World War II, and, in Russia, comparing someone to Hitler is the ultimate blasphemy. An enraged Putin plotted his payback. In June 2015, just as Hillary was gearing up for another run at the White House, Putin ordered the GRU, the main intelligence directorate of the Russian military, to begin hacking the computers of the Democratic National Committee.

■　■　■

When Putin issued that order to the GRU, he could not have known that Donald Trump—who was dismissed at the time as a joke by the media and by many members of his own party—would capture the Republican presidential nomination. During the first several months of the Russian disinformation campaign in the United States, Putin concentrated entirely on Hillary and ignored Trump. He believed like everyone else that Hillary would win the White House, and he focused on undermining her future presidency.

"As for the Trump-Putin conspiracy story, I never believed it," said a highly informed source in Washington who had access to secret intelligence information. "If Trump and members of his campaign team had such great contacts with the Kremlin, why did they bother to speak with [Russian Ambassador Sergey] Kislyak, who is not from the inner Kremlin circle around Putin? If you have all these special contacts with Putin, you don't go to someone like Kislyak, who is a garden-variety diplomat, a nice man, but not from Putin's inner circle. You go directly to Putin or his cronies. But there is no proof that that's what occurred. What all this tells me is that Trump never had a special relationship with Putin in the first place."

Nonetheless, many people jumped on the Russian collusion story as a means to take Trump down. Among the villains in this campaign was Senator Al Franken, the former *Saturday Night Live* comic, whose snide remarks about Trump helped raise his national profile among Democrats and earned him buzz as a potential presidential candidate in 2020. Appearing on *Real Time with Bill Maher*, Franken was asked whether impeachment proceedings might be brought against Trump. "Let me remind you again that Republicans are in the majority," said Franken, "so I think it'll be—it's months and months away."

At a Senate Judiciary Committee hearing on May 3, 2017, Franken asked FBI Director James Comey to explain why the U.S. intelligence community had concluded that Russia favored Trump over Hillary in the election.

"The intelligence communities' assessment had a couple of parts with respect to that," Comey said. "One is [Trump] wasn't Hillary Clinton, who Putin hated and wanted to harm in any possible way, and so [Trump] was her opponent, so necessarily they supported him. And then, also this second notion that the intelligence community assessed that Putin believed he would be more able to make deals, reach agreements with someone with a business background than with someone who'd grown up in more of a government environment."

Franken couldn't resist volunteering his own conspiracy theory.

"Okay," he said, "well, I'm curious about just how closely Russia followed the Kremlin playbook when it [meddled] in our democracy, specifically whether the Russians had a preference for President Trump because he had already been ensnared in their web of patronage—web of patronage is a quote from the I.C.'s [intelligence community's] report."

Comey looked across the room at the blustering senator and set him straight. "That," said Comey, "was *not* the basis for the I.C.'s assessment."

In fact, the Russia story was a scandal without a crime. After months of investigations, no one had produced a shred of evidence that either Donald Trump or any member of his campaign had colluded with the Russians.

3

THE ROOM OF REQUIREMENT

The Judge had just come home from church and was about to sit down with his family for Sunday dinner when his secure, encrypted telephone rang.

A clerk at the Foreign Intelligence Surveillance Court informed him that an urgent matter of national security, brought before the court by the Department of Justice, required his immediate attention.

The FISA court, as it is known, oversees requests for surveillance warrants by federal law enforcement and intelligence agencies against foreign spies and agents of foreign powers operating inside the United States. It is open 24/7 in the event of a national emergency, and one of eleven circuit court judges appointed by the Chief Justice of the Supreme Court is always on duty. Today that responsibility fell on the shoulders of this Judge, whose identity cannot be disclosed because everything connected to the Foreign Intelligence Surveillance Court is top secret.

The Judge put on his go-to-church suit jacket, and climbed into a car that was driven by an armed guard. The traffic was light, and it took them only a few minutes to arrive at the E. Barrett Prettyman Courthouse, a hulking limestone structure on Connecticut Avenue and Third Street.

There, waiting for the Judge in the lobby, were two attorneys from the Department of Justice. The three men got into an elevator. When they got off, they walked down a long corridor to an unmarked door. The Judge used the biometric hand-scanner to identify himself and gain entrance to the soundproof courtroom, which was an SCIF, or a Sensitive Compartmented Information Facility. The building's employees jokingly referred to it as the Room of Requirement, a reference to the magical room that "comes and goes" in *Harry Potter and the Order of the Phoenix*.

It was a small, cramped space with just enough room for a raised judge's bench, a stenographer, and seating for a dozen or so government attorneys. There was no jury box, because the court always sat *ex parte*—that is, it conducted its secret business in the absence of the public.

The Judge went into his chambers to study the government's application for a warrant. The National Security Agency had information that Russia's military intelligence directorate had hacked the computers of the DNC and breached the Gmail account of John Podesta, the chairman of Hillary Clinton's campaign.

"The application took him by surprise," said a recently retired FISA Court judge, who was familiar with the case and was interviewed for this book. "As its name implies, the FISA Court overseas surveillance warrants for foreigners, not Americans, but the main focus of the application was clearly Donald Trump and his campaign's alleged ties to the Russians.

"The request for surveillance specifically named Trump and three of his properties—Trump Tower, the Trump golf club in New Jersey, and Mar-a-Lago," the retired FISA judge continued. "It requested permission to intercept the electronic records from two Russian banks that had communicated with the Internet address of a computer server in Trump Tower."

While still in his chambers, the Judge asked his clerk to set up a conference call with several other FISA Court judges. When they were all on the line, he read them the passages in the application that worried him the most. The other judges agreed that the application did not rise to the level of an urgent request, because there was no evidence of a national emergency and, for that matter, no proof that Donald Trump was connected to Russian espionage. The application was an egregious effort to damage Trump.

The Judge emerged from his chambers and told the waiting Department of Justice lawyers that their filing didn't meet the standards of an imminent danger to the security of the United States.

"This," he told them, "is not an emergency. I'm scheduling a hearing for later this week."

And with that, he returned to his chambers, disrobed, and went back home to eat his Sunday dinner.

4

REVERSE INTELLIGENCE

A t ten o'clock in the morning on the day appointed by the Judge, Sally Quillian Yates, the deputy attorney general of the United States, stepped out of a black Chevrolet Suburban in front of the E. Barrett Prettyman Courthouse. A slim, smartly dressed woman of fifty-six, who looked years younger than her age, she wheeled a weighty legal briefcase. A cavalcade of other Suburbans pulled up behind her and out stepped more than a dozen attorneys representing the FBI, the Department of Justice, the CIA, the Director of National Intelligence, and the National Security Agency.

Yates was steeped in the law: her grandfather, grandmother, brother, and father[1] were all lawyers, and over the past thirty years she had assembled an impressive résumé. As the U.S. Attorney for the Northern District of Georgia, she successfully prosecuted Eric Rudolph, the Olympic Park bomber, putting him behind bars for life. She and her husband were lifelong Democrats who had contributed to Barack Obama's presidential campaign, and in 2015 Obama appointed her deputy attorney general, placing her in day-to-day charge of the 116,000 employees at the Justice Department. She was not a fan of Donald Trump.

Yates was used to winning cases, and as she and her colleagues stepped into the elevator, she had every reason to believe that obtaining the FISA warrant, which had been signed by her boss, Attorney General Loretta Lynch, would be a slam dunk. More than 98 percent of the government's applications were approved by the FISA Court.

After Yates and her colleagues took their seats in the courtroom, the Judge appeared and asked to hear their oral arguments. He sharply questioned the government's lawyers, who requested approval for "electronic surveillance, physical search and other investigative actions" of the activities of two Russian banks and of any "U.S. person" connected to the investigation.

As the Judge pressed the lawyers for answers, it became clear that the surveillance of any "U.S. person" covered Donald Trump and four of his associates: Lieutenant General Michael Flynn, the former head of the Defense Intelligence Agency and Trump's adviser on national security affairs; campaign manager Paul Manafort, who had been involved in investment projects with a Russian oligarch close to Putin; Carter Page, an informal adviser on foreign affairs who, wittingly or not, was in touch with Russian agents while he visited Moscow; and Roger Stone, a political strategist who some believed had contacts with a hacker working for Russian intelligence.

The Judge retreated to his chambers and placed another conference call to his FISA Court colleagues. To many of them, it appeared that the government was being less than candid about the motive for its request. It was asking for permission to monitor suspected communications between foreign banks and a Trump Organization computer, but it was obviously seeking a backdoor way—known in CIA-ese as "reverse intelligence"—to monitor the activities of American citizens, including one Donald J. Trump, who was running for president.

The Judge was gone from the courtroom for about an hour, and when he returned, he announced that he was rejecting the government's application for a warrant. The application had to be modified so that it did not appear that the government was indulging in reverse intelligence.

Loud groans filled the courtroom.

The Judge was not pleased by the outburst. He rose from the bench and scowled at the lawyers.

"Your Honor! Your Honor!" the desperate government lawyers shouted after him as he disappeared into his chambers.

5

MOMENTOUS
CONSEQUENCES

That same day, Attorney General Loretta Lynch called Valerie Jarrett to give her the bad news about the FISA Court's action.[1]

The Department of Justice was already reeling from another controversy. A few days before, Lynch had been forced to step aside from the Hillary Clinton email investigation because of a major blunder: she had met with Bill Clinton on her private plane on the tarmac at Phoenix International Airport.

When the story of the meeting broke in the press, it gave rise to charges that the fix was in, that the administration was conspiring to protect Hillary Clinton from the FBI's investigation. The badly compromised Lynch stepped aside from the Hillary email investigation and agreed to accept the recommendation of FBI Director James Comey of whether Hillary should be prosecuted. Comey's decision not to press charges against Hillary, even though she and her colleagues had been "extremely careless in the handling of classified information," and even though it appeared obvious that she had broken the law, remained a black mark on his reputation.[2]

Jarrett was personally fond of Lynch and asked her how she was holding up against the firestorm of criticism. The fact was, Lynch had sunk into a deep depression. She acknowledged that meeting with Bill Clinton had been a mistake, and she was full of remorse and shame and was having trouble concentrating on her job.

Jarrett sympathized but had another pressing issue on which she needed Lynch's help. She told Lynch that the president wanted to bypass the FISA Court for the time being. They could go back to the FISA Court with a modified application later in the fall, Jarrett said. In the meantime, she wanted Lynch to speak to Carl Ghattas, the head of the National Security Branch of the Justice Department, which had oversight over the FBI's counter-intelligence operations. Jarrett wanted an FBI counter-intelligence investigation into Russia's meddling in the election, and she wanted Lynch to order Ghattas to give Comey that authority. More than that, she wanted the FBI to investigate the possibility that members of the Trump campaign had cooperated with the Kremlin's dirty work.

Lynch did as she was told and Comey unleashed his agents toward the end of July 2016, fewer than one hundred days before the November election. Though the agents found no evidence of collusion between the Trump campaign and the Russians, the investigations would still have momentous consequences.

6

300 BLOWS

"There's a level of brutality in boxing," Donald Trump told me. "It's hard to take 300 punches in the face and come back for another round. I remember hearing a champ after a fight say to the cameras, 'I want to thank the Lord my savior, who gave me the ability to beat the shit out of my opponent.'"

My conversation with Trump took place almost twenty-five years ago when I was traveling around the country with him, researching a story for *Vanity Fair*. His comment on the brutality of boxing came to mind while I was putting together this book, which is about the opponents who are trying for a knockout punch against President Trump.

At the time of my magazine assignment—toward the end of 1993—Trump was agonizing over whether to marry a five-foot-eight-inch former beauty queen, model, and showgirl named Marla Maples, who was the mother of his baby daughter Tiffany. He had just dug himself out of a massive financial hole—at one point he owed the banks nearly

$1 billion—and he was nervous about his plan to take his Atlantic City casinos public.

Trump's comment about boxing was a metaphor for the beating he was taking in the press for his soap opera divorce from Ivana, the mother of Donald Jr., Eric, and Ivanka; the bruising negotiations he was having with Marla over a prenuptial agreement;[1] and, most painful of all, the grief he was getting from his parents, who opposed his marriage to Marla.

"Ivana still loves you," his eighty-year-old Scottish-born mother Mary MacLeod Trump told him over a Sunday brunch that I attended with Trump and his parents in the Palm Court of the Plaza Hotel. "She'd take you back."

"I know," said Trump. "I talk to her all the time. At least a couple of times a week. Ivana can't feel great about my baby with Marla. She can't be thinking, 'Isn't this wonderful.'"

Trump hated talking about marriage; he referred to it as "the big *M* word." But he couldn't avoid it, for sitting across the table from him was his eighty-nine-year-old father, Fred Trump, whom he idolized and who told him that he should stick with Ivana and keep Marla as a mistress "on the Q.T."

In the end, Trump married Marla in an opulent wedding at the Plaza, which I attended, and my piece ran on the cover of *Vanity Fair* with the headline "Trump Family Values." The story corroborated Trump's claim, which the press continued to discount, that he had achieved a spectacular financial comeback and was on his way to becoming a billionaire. It also laid bare the lurid details of Trump's rocky relationship with Marla.

"They might love each other," I wrote, "but they enjoyed torturing each other, too. Donald complained that Marla didn't show him sufficient appreciation for what he had done for her—making her a celebrity and giving her the good life.... Marla knew how to push Donald's buttons. She taunted him in public for being overweight. She played with the hair on his head, lifting it up and exposing his scalp, and poking fun at his efforts to hide his hair loss. She derided his sexual prowess in front of his friends and associates."

After Trump read the story, he phoned me.

I braced for the worst.

"I loved your story!" he said. "It was great! You are the first journalist to write that the Trumpster is back!"

■ ■ ■

Among the many things his enemies always seem to get wrong about Trump is his ability to come back from a beating. It is true that his ego is easily bruised, but during his race for the White House—nineteen walloping months in the ring, to use his boxing trope—he took 300 punches in the face and still "beat the shit out of" his opponents.

Journalists dug through their college history books to find an American politician who had been as reviled as Trump. The name they kept coming up with was Andrew Jackson, the seventh president of the United States.

"In a conversation with Daniel Webster in 1824," noted Michael Kruse, an award-winning staff writer at the *Tampa Bay Times*, "Thomas Jefferson described Jackson as 'one of the most unfit men I know of' to become president of the United States, 'a dangerous man' who cannot speak in a civilized manner because he 'choke[s] with rage,' a man whose 'passions are terrible.' Jefferson feared that the slightest insult from a foreign leader would impel Jackson to declare war."

Trump didn't have a Thomas Jefferson to contend with, but he did have plenty of villainous enemies—the Never-Trump crowd in the Republican Party, the media, Hollywood stars and moguls, late-night talk-show hosts, corporate America, college professors, many gays, blacks, and Latinos, and the billion-dollar Hillary Clinton political machine.

His enemies called him every name in the book—a racist, a sexist, an Islamophobe, a homophobe, a transphobe, a xenophobe, a white supremacist, a Nazi, a fascist, a misogynist, an idiot, an ignoramus, a self-promoter, an authoritarian, a blowhard, a jackass, a dummy, a scum, a snake-oil salesman, and on and on.

They said he was nuts, that he displayed the classic traits of a mental illness called narcissistic personality disorder. They said he was a Dr.

Strangelove who would destroy decades of U.S. foreign policy, and start World War III. And they said his candidacy was a joke. Charles M. Blow, a columnist for the *New York Times*, wrote, "Donald Trump has virtually stopped trying to win this election by any conventional metric and is instead stacking logs of grievance on the funeral pyre with the great anticipation of setting it ablaze, if current polls turn out to be predictive."

What the pollsters—and journalists like Blow—failed to understand was that Trump was the only politician in either party who listened to the voices of marginalized Americans and promised to become their tribune. He didn't have to bamboozle anybody. Common-sense Americans saw his many flaws. And yet, tens of millions of them were willing to overlook his impulsive, sometimes infantile, often self-defeating behavior because they believed he would make their lives better.

"There are signs of hope for fresh thinking in both the U.S. and the U.K.," wrote Conrad Black, the controversial Canadian press lord. "Donald Trump horrifies Canadians as a caricature of the Ugly American of the 1950s vintage: loud, boastful, boorish, ignorant, obscenely materialistic, and illiberal in every respect, as nauseating a personality as he is reassuring to us of our comparative civility, culture, and equability, our inoffensiveness and niceness, if not exactly our style. There is some reason for this judgment of Trump from what we have generally seen of him in public now for 30 years.

"[The] fact that he is doing so well," Black continued, "must be taken not as a sign of the triumph of the belligerent, clumsy, bullying America the world knows and dislikes, but rather as indicative of the rage of scores of millions of Americans as they work themselves to the bone to stumble from pay cheque to pay cheque with maxed-out credit cards and loud rumors of recession.

"They are angry about rising crime rates, the many thousands of American lives and trillions of dollars that have been squandered in the Middle East to produce an appalling humanitarian crisis, the debasement of the currency and the reduction of their great country to the status of a laughing stock. These are legitimate grievances and for Trump to stare at audiences with an Ozymandian curled lip and say… 'I love the poorly educated people,' to applause…only means that he knew how angry the people were and knew how to give voice to that anger, to be its evocator and its voice."

■   ■   ■

I witnessed firsthand how Trump related to voters when I flew with him to his rallies in the American Heartland during the Republican primaries.

"A lot of reporters have asked to travel on my plane, including Bob Woodward," Trump said when he invited me to fly with him, "and I've told them all no. You are the first reporter on my plane. Just so you know—I'm treating you special."

We had known each other for more than thirty years, but in classic Trump fashion he needed to remind me that in his world—the ruthless world of real estate developers—everything was a transaction. He expected something in return for treating me as special. I made no promises, and he had no advance knowledge of what I would write about him.

Trump traveled light. He was accompanied by Steve Miller, his rail-thin, thirty-one-year-old policy wonk, who handed him printouts of the latest Internet news and called him "Mr. Trump," never "Donald"; Dan Scavino Jr., forty, who handled his Twitter account and always showed him the tweets before they were sent out so that Trump could edit them, which he frequently did; and Keith Schiller, his long-time personal bodyguard, who was in charge of his traveling wardrobe, which fit into a single large suitcase. Hope Hicks, his twenty-eight-year-old spokeswoman, was at a funeral for a family member and couldn't make the trip.

Stories about his rallies typically portrayed his supporters as a ragtag army of bigoted white male rednecks who came from a broken America: these people were in trouble financially, their families were being destroyed by drugs, and they felt that their country was being stolen from them by the politically correct.

When I arrived at my first rally, I half expected to see people who looked like the dispossessed Okies in the movie *The Grapes of Wrath*.

Instead, when Trump stepped out on the platform to deliver his speech, he faced a sunny, neatly dressed crowd of men and women, many of whom brought along their kids for a fun family outing. They wore "Make America Great Again" hats and T-shirts and carried "Build the Wall" and "Lock Her Up" placards.

Trump spoke from notes that he had scribbled with a Sharpie on a folded piece of paper while traveling in his plane. But mostly he spoke off the cuff. He told them they were the "forgotten Americans." They were being cheated by foreigners who outsmarted "our dumb leaders" and stole away millions of American jobs. They were being screwed by elitists who lived on the East and West coasts and ran Washington, and who had become rich at their expense. These elitists, who looked down their noses at the rest of America, had shattered the American Dream.

It was a bleak picture, but Trump promised a rosy future. If he became president, he would put people over politicians in Washington. "You won't be forgotten any more, I can promise you that," he said. He would build a wall—"and make Mexico pay for it"—and he would stop the drugs and crime that were spilling over America's southern border. He would bring back jobs. He would make America safe again, respected again, great again. He would make them all winners.

As I watched the expressions on the faces in the crowd, I was reminded of another rally I had attended years before. It was 1957; I was a copy boy and feature writer at the *New York Daily News*, and I was assigned to cover Billy Graham's first Madison Square Garden crusade. A huge crowd turned out to hear the evangelist preach about Sodom and Gomorrah. Graham substituted "New York" for the names of those sinful cities, and he prayed that New York would "have a spiritual resurrection." At the end of the rally, hundreds of people stood up and, as if in a collective trance, came forward to answer Graham's call to be born again.

Something similar—if entirely secular—happened at Trump rallies. Judging by the ecstatic look on the faces in his crowds, Trump spoke to a spiritual yearning for an American revival. Trump's supporters felt that while elites prospered, America itself—its basis, its soul, as a land of opportunity, as a unique culture—was being lost. Trump, they thought, was the one man who fully recognized this threat—and the one man who had the gumption and the ability to actually do something about it.

Everyone—the media, the pollsters, Hillary Clinton's campaign advisers, and all the other villains who didn't want to see Trump succeed—missed the fact that Americans were responding to Trump's call for a remedy to modern evils.

7

WISHFUL THINKING

Other politicians would have given their eyeteeth to get away with half the things Trump said during the campaign.

"He's a war hero because he was captured. I like people that weren't captured, okay?" That was Trump talking about Senator John McCain at the Family Leadership Summit in Ames, Iowa.

Or take this Trumpism: "You could see there was blood coming out of her eyes, blood coming out of her wherever." Trump talking about Megyn Kelly.

Or: "I know more about ISIS than the generals do. Believe me."

Or: "I could stand in the middle of Fifth Avenue and shoot somebody and I wouldn't lose voters."

Or: "[Putin] called me a genius. I like him so far, I have to tell you."

Or: "Do I look [like] a president? How handsome am I, right? How handsome."

Or: "Russia, if you're listening, I hope you're able to find the 30,000 [Hillary] emails that are missing. I think you will be rewarded mightily by our press."

Or: "This was locker room banter, a private conversation that took place many years ago. Bill Clinton has said far worse to me on the golf course—not even close."[1]

That last quote was Trump's response to widespread public outrage following the leak of a video in which he boasted about taking sexual advantage of women. In the eleven-year-old video footage, which pro-Hillary executives at NBC News leaked to the *Washington Post* on the eve of the presidential election, Trump regaled Billy Bush of *Access Hollywood* about his failed attempt to seduce Nancy O'Dell, Bush's co-host on the syndicated tabloid show.

"I moved on her and I failed," Trump was heard saying in the hot-mike incident. "I'll admit it. I did try and fuck her. She was married. And I moved on her very heavily. In fact, I took her out furniture shopping. She wanted to get some furniture. I said, 'I'll show you where they have some nice furniture.' I took her out furniture—I moved on her like a bitch. But I couldn't get there. And she was married. Then all of a sudden I see her, she's now got the big phony tits and everything. She's totally changed her look."

In a later segment of the tape, Trump talked in a similar manner about Arianne Zucker, a soap opera actress, whom he and Bush were about to meet.

"I better use some Tic Tacs just in case I start kissing her," Trump said. "You know I'm automatically attracted to beautiful—I just start kissing them. It's like a magnet. Just kiss. I don't even wait. And when you're a star, they let you do it. You can do anything. Grab 'em by the pussy. You can do anything."

Nothing Trump had said before—not his ridicule of John McCain's wartime heroism, not his put-down of a Gold Star family at the Democratic National Convention—caused a bigger backlash than his "Grab 'em by the pussy" remark. No presidential candidate had ever been heard talking like that because none ever had—at least within the realm of a microphone.

Republicans ran for the exits. Speaker Paul Ryan canceled a joint appearance with Trump in Wisconsin, and told his House colleagues: "I am not going to defend Donald Trump—not now, not in the future." Senator McCain, who had never hidden his hatred of Trump, declared: "No woman should ever be victimized by this kind of inappropriate behavior. He alone bears the burden of his conduct and alone should suffer the consequences."

"I don't know how you recover from something like that," said Alfonso Aguilar, the president of the Latino Partnership for Conservative Principles. "But I think all Republicans must come out now and denounce him forcefully and call on him to withdraw. He cannot remain the party standard-bearer after those comments."

The media had a field day with the crude *Access Hollywood* tape.

"It's fitting," wrote *Politico* reporters Glenn Thrush and Katie Glueck, "that the election of Hillary Clinton as the first female president might have been sealed by Donald Trump's treatment of women as subordinate, interchangeable, pliable playthings."

Along with the rest of the media, *Politico* speculated that the release of the videotape would turn out to be Trump's "coup de grace," the moment he plunged into a "final death spiral."

But like so many other "fatal" scandals that were supposed to discredit Trump and force him out of the race, this one failed to stick. His followers discounted his vulgarities. As far as they were concerned, his behavior only proved that he was the real thing—wrong on comportment but right on substance. More important than Trump's "locker room banter," in their opinion, was whom he would nominate to the Supreme Court, his position on border control, and the rest of his populist, nationalist, conservative agenda. They believed in what he stood for.

The same could not be said of the media's reputation for accuracy, which took a huge hit during the presidential campaign. The *New York Times*, under its left-leaning executive editor, Dean Baquet, gave Hillary an 85 percent chance of winning the election. Fifteen days before the election the *Washington Post*, under its executive editor Martin Baron, declared: "Donald Trump's chances of winning are approaching zero."

The media's incessant obituaries of Trump—like so much of their other reporting—turned out to be based on nothing more than partisan wishful thinking.

8

ABE ROSENTHAL IS
TURNING IN HIS GRAVE

A month before the election, WikiLeaks produced proof of what had long been obvious—many members of the media conspired during the campaign against Trump and colluded with Hillary Clinton. Indeed, among the villains who emerged during the campaign, perhaps none did more damage to themselves than members of the media.

Take the case of *Politico's* senior staff writer, Glenn Thrush, a voguish figure in the Washington press corps. According to a trove of hacked John Podesta emails, Thrush was in cahoots with the chairman of Hillary's campaign. Podesta was an intimidating figure to many reporters; he was notorious for his hot temper, and when he blew his fuse, which he did on frequent occasions, reporters said that he turned into his Evil Twin Skippy. At one point, Glenn Thrush asked "Skippy" for approval of the language in a story he was writing—a journalistic no-no second only to plagiarism.

"Because I have become a hack I will send u the whole section that pertains to u," Thrush emailed Podesta. "Please don't share or tell anyone I did this. Tell me if I fucked up anything."

Thrush wasn't the only Hillary Clinton sycophant in the media. After he interviewed Hillary, Mark Leibovich, the chief national correspondent of the *New York Times Magazine*, emailed Jennifer Palmieri, Hillary's director of communications, offering her quote approval and promising her that she "could veto what you don't want." This violated a *New York Times* policy forbidding its reporters to give news sources approval of quotations in stories. Palmieri asked Leibovich to leave out a joke about Sarah Palin cooking mouse stew. When Leibovich's story appeared, the Palin joke was gone from his copy.

Another *Times* reporter, John Harwood, who also served as the chief Washington correspondent for CNBC, had a backdoor relationship with the Clinton campaign. In several emails to Podesta, Harwood praised Hillary's performance, offered advice on how to deal with Ben Carson if he became the Republican presidential nominee, and criticized his own newspaper for collaborating with Peter Schweizer on his bestseller, *Clinton Cash*. Harwood was a moderator at a Republican presidential debate, and afterward he bragged to Podesta in an email how he had sandbagged Trump with a trick question: "Let's be honest, is this a comic book version of a presidential campaign?"

But it didn't take the WikiLeaks email dump to prove that most journalists were biased against Trump. Their contempt for the Republican nominee was there in plain sight on social media.

"News reporters are supposed to keep their opinions out of stories they write and air," noted Paul Farhi, the *Washington Post's* media reporter. "Twitter, it seems, is another realm entirely. With the political campaigns staggering into their final days, mainstream reporters otherwise obliged to objectivity—or at least a reasonably balanced, non-argumentative account of events—have taken to Twitter to unburden themselves of their apparently true feelings about the race."

"[Trump was] really just asking for it with this venue," tweeted Alex Burns of the *New York Times* after Trump gave a speech in

Gettysburg, Pennsylvania. "Like a losing caucus candidate speaking in Waterloo, Iowa."

Glenn Thrush, who was eventually hired away from *Politico* by the *New York Times* despite his incriminating Podesta email, was openly snarky about Trump on Twitter. During a live presidential debate, Thrush tweeted: "Note to future presidential hopefuls: debate prep, maybe, matters a little" and "The problem for Trump: [Hillary] is better at being reasonable than he is."

Charlie Warzel, *BuzzFeed*'s technology writer, went a lot further than that. After the Trump-Pence logo was shown for the first time, Warzel tweeted: "lol to all of us tho for thinking that after a year of racist, vitriolic campaigning that trump gives two shits about a logo."

■ ■ ■

"The mainstream media is going to need to go through a serious readjustment period after this presidential election," wrote the *Washington Times*' Kelly Riddell. "The collusion between reporters and the Clinton campaign, revealed by WikiLeaks, has laid bare to the American public the left-leaning bias of the press."

Jim Rutenberg, the media columnist for the *New York Times*, didn't agree. Rutenberg, whose penseés on journalism influenced the thinking of other reporters, argued that journalists should abandon their quest for objectivity when it came to covering Donald Trump.

"If you're a working journalist and you believe that Donald J. Trump is a demagogue playing to the nation's worst racist and nationalistic tendencies, that he cozies up to anti-American dictators and that he would be dangerous with control of the United States nuclear codes, how the heck are you supposed to cover him?" wrote Rutenberg.

"Because if you believe all of those things," he continued, "you have to throw out the textbook American journalism has been using for the better part of the past half-century, if not longer, and approach it in a way you've never approached anything in your career. If you view a Trump presidency as something that's potentially dangerous, then your reporting is going to reflect that. You would move closer than you've ever been to being oppositional. That's uncomfortable and uncharted territory for every mainstream, non-opinion journalist I've ever known, and by normal standards, untenable.... But let's face it: Balance has been on vacation since Mr. Trump stepped onto his golden Trump Tower escalator last year to announce his candidacy."

Many journalists were quick to embrace Rutenberg's new guidelines. Among them was Joe Scarborough, the co-host of MSNBC's *Morning Joe,* who had gone from being cozy with Trump to being his foe.

"How balanced do you have to be when one side is irrational?" Scarborough said when questioned about his on-air attacks on Trump.

Perhaps no news organization was more hostile to Trump than the *Washington Post*, which under the ownership of Amazon's Jeff Bezos had gone off the partisan rails. Here are some of the *Post*'s most outrageous online headlines.

- "This 30-Second Video Is Absolutely Devastating for Donald Trump"
- "Trump's Shallowness Runs Deep"
- "Donald Trump Is Suffering From Mushroom Breath"
- "The Unbearable Stench of Trump's B.S."

Not to be outdone by its chief rival, the *New York Times* released a three-minute video, "Voices from Donald Trump's Rallies, Uncensored," that began with a trigger warning: "This video includes vulgarities and racial and ethnic slurs." The video depicted Trump supporters as religious bigots and fascists. One wore a T-shirt with the words "Fuck Islam." Another displayed a button that read, "KFC Hillary Special—two fat thighs, two small breasts...left wing."

■ ■ ■

"The media and Democrats are so close in association and so close in their philosophical views that we might as well use one word to describe both, and that's Mediacrats," Texas Representative Lamar Smith, a fifteen-term lawmaker, told the *Washington Examiner*'s Paul Bedard. "How can the media be considered 'mainstream' when it doesn't represent a majority of the American people? It's more accurate to use the term 'liberal.' [The media] want themselves to be the oracle. They themselves want to be the only conduit. They themselves want to tell the American people what to think. I am concerned that it is hurting our republic."

"Swaths of the media do have a credibility problem with much of the public," Daniel Henninger, the deputy editorial page editor of the *Wall Street Journal*, agreed. "But that no longer matters, because many media platforms have decided to set aside nominal standards of objectivity and turn partisanship and resistance into a business model, pitching their coverage to half the electorate and ignoring the rest as commercially irrelevant.

"Mr. Trump keeps saying they should thank him because he's building their audiences," Henninger continued. "This misrepresents what is taking place now. They are turning the angry Trump tweets…into pure political entertainment for their customers. They will make Donald Trump their tweeting dancing bear, if he lets them."

Not all members of the media were blind to the threat posed by leftist reporters and editors. As far back as 2004, Daniel Okrent, the public editor of the *New York Times*, asked, "Is the New York Times a Liberal Newspaper?" He answered his own question in four words: "Of course it is."

"My concern is the flammable stuff that ignites the right," wrote Okrent. "These are the social issues: gay rights, gun control, abortion and environmental regulations, among others. And if you think the *Times* plays it down the middle on any of them, you've been reading the paper with your eyes closed. But if you're examining the paper's coverage of these subjects from a perspective that is neither urban nor Northeastern nor culturally seen-it-all; if you are among the groups the *Times* treats as strange objects to be examined on a laboratory slide (devout Catholics, gun owners, Orthodox Jews, Texans); if your value system wouldn't wear well on a composite *New York Times* journalist, then a walk through this paper can make you feel you're traveling in a strange and forbidding world."

After Okrent's *j'accuse*, some people held out hope that the editors of the *Times* would rethink their news coverage. But according to Liz Spayd, who followed Okrent twelve years later as the paper's public editor, the *Times* remained relentlessly liberal.

"Like the tiresome bore at a party," wrote Spayd, "I went around asking several journalists in the newsroom about…claims that the *Times* sways to the left. Mostly I was met with a roll of the eyes. All sides hate us, they said. We're tough on everyone. That's nothing new here.

"That response may be tempting," Spayd continued, "but unless the strategy is to become *The New Republic* gone daily, [the] perception [of leftist bias] by many readers strikes me as poison. A paper whose journalism appeals to only half the country has a dangerously severed public mission. And a news organization trying to survive off revenues from readers shouldn't erase American conservatives from its list of prospects."[1]

■ ■ ■

When I read Liz Spayd's indictment of the *Times*, I was reminded of a conversation about journalistic ethics that I had forty years ago when I was hired as the editor-in-chief of the *New York Times Magazine* by A.M. Rosenthal, the paper's executive editor. During Abe's time at the helm of the *Times* (1977–1987), the paper's newsroom leaned to the left, and he cautioned his editors to be on guard against reporters whose ideas had been shaped by the free-speech movement, the civil rights movement, the anti-Vietnam war movement, and Watergate. He was especially wary of reporters who got too close to their sources.

"I don't care if you fuck an elephant," Abe liked to say, "just so long as you don't cover the circus."

Abe died in 2006 and the epitaph on his tombstone reads: "He kept the paper straight." If he read today's *New York Times*, Abe Rosenthal would be turning in his grave.

9

FIT TO BE PRESIDENT?

Bill Clinton got the news from Chelsea: her mother had stumbled and collapsed in front of dozens of people at the September 11 memorial service at Ground Zero. She was trying to pull herself together at Chelsea's apartment in the Flatiron District of Manhattan.

"She had to be carried by the Secret Service into the van," Chelsea said, according to someone who overheard her conversation. "When they dragged her [into the van], she lost a shoe."

Bill urged Chelsea to get Hillary to a hospital as quickly as possible.

"She won't go," Chelsea said. "Nick [Merrill, Hillary's campaign spokesman] says she's got to show reporters she's okay."

Hillary needed to have a thorough medical examination, Bill insisted.

"I told her that," Chelsea said, "but she says [if she goes to a hospital] it'll get out [in public] and be the end [of her campaign]."

■ ■ ■

At noon, Hillary emerged from her daughter's apartment. She was alone—there was no sign of the ever-present Huma Abedin or any other campaign aide. She was sending a message: she could stand on her own two feet. She was wearing a pair of round blue-tinted glasses that were vaguely reminiscent of the kind of glasses John Lennon used to wear.

"How are you feeling?" one of the waiting reporters shouted.

"I'm feeling great," said Hillary.

"What happened? What happened?" the reporters yelled.

Hillary shrugged and seemed at a loss for words.

At last she said, "It's a beautiful day in New York."

"What happened? What happened?"

She ignored the questions and got into her Chevrolet Suburban and sped away, leaving the reporters behind.

■ ■ ■

Shortly after she arrived at her home in Chappaqua, she received a call from Valerie Jarrett.

"The president and Michelle are very concerned about you," Jarrett said, according to a source who spoke with Jarrett afterward. "They think you should have a checkup at Bethesda [The Walter Reed National Military Medical Center]. They'll make the arrangements."

Hillary laughed off the suggestion.

"I'm fine," she said. "I'll be fine."

■ ■ ■

But she wasn't fine.

For the past two years—in my books, *Blood Feud* and *Unlikeable,* and on my blog, *Ed Klein Confidential*—I had been reporting about Hillary's failing health. The mainstream media ridiculed my reporting as a rightwing hit job, but campaign manager Robby Mook knew better. His worst nightmare had always been that Hillary would collapse in public and reveal the truth about her medical condition. Mook had encouraged Hillary to denounce Donald Trump as "unfit to be president." Now, her collapse on 9/11 turned that question on its head: Was *she* fit to be president?

At first, her campaign tried to make light of her collapse. Nick Merrill said that Hillary was "dehydrated" and felt "overheated" at the commemoration ceremony. That was a lie. Later that day, Hillary's personal physician, Dr. Lisa Bardack, released a statement that Hillary had been experiencing a cough related to allergies, and that she was suffering from pneumonia. That was only partly true.

Hillary was suffering from arrhythmia (an abnormal heartbeat), a leaking heart valve, chronic low blood pressure, insufficient blood flow, a tendency to form life-threatening blood clots, and troubling side effects from her medications.

She paid secret visits to the New York Presbyterian Hospital, where she arrived through a private entrance out of public sight and where she could rely on her doctors' discretion not to speak to the media.

Her doctors prescribed Coumadin (a blood thinner) and a beta blocker to treat her arrhythmia and heart-valve problem. However, these medications had the side effect of making her drowsy and tired and lowering her blood pressure, which led to frequent bouts of light-headedness and fainting spells.

In addition to the 9/11 incident, Hillary had suffered three other fainting spells that the public was aware of.

- She fainted in 2005 during an appearance before a women's group in Buffalo
- She fainted in 2009 while boarding her plane in Yemen, where she fell and fractured her elbow
- She fainted in her office at the State Department in 2012, hit her head, suffered a concussion, and developed a blood clot between her brain and skull

After her 2012 concussion, Hillary had trouble with her vision and had to wear corrective Fresnel prism lenses, which gave rise to questions about the long-term seriousness of her condition. Bill Clinton revealed that it took Hillary "six months of very serious work" to recuperate from her concussion. And in one of the emails released by the State Department from Hillary's private server, Huma Abedin confessed that Hillary was easily "confused."

In addition to Hillary's publicly known fainting spells, there were other incidents that had been kept from the public. For example, after her eleven-hour testimony before the Trey Gowdy Benghazi committee, Hillary swooned as she walked to her waiting car. She had to be carried by her aides and hauled bodily into the back seat.

Among Hillary's friends, it was common knowledge that she suffered from tension headaches, fell asleep while studying her speeches, got dizzy, and frequently stumbled and fell at her home in Chappaqua.

"She looks to me to be in absolute agony a lot of the time, particularly after she's been on the campaign for a long period of time," one of Hillary's friends said. "The campaign people are aware of the problem and are doing everything to make her schedule as easy as possible. Huma often brings her a cool wet towel, which Hillary applies to her forehead and neck. Huma kneels down, whispers to her, rubs her shoulders and comforts her."

■　■　■

Hillary's collapse at Ground Zero unnerved Democrats.

"Rumors [are] flying that top DNC officials are considering alternate plans in case Clinton is unable to finish out the campaign," reported Louise Mensch of *Heat Street*, a libertarian website owned by News Corp.

"Bill is nervous, a little paranoid in my opinion, that the chatter about dumping Hillary from the ticket may actually develop into something," one of Bill Clinton's advisers said in an interview for this book. "He says it's just a far-out precaution, but he wants to have in place a team of lawyers who can fight back hard against any move in that direction.

"I've made some preliminary calls to attorneys who are election-law specialists," the adviser continued. "I have a call in to [former U.S. solicitor general] Ted Olson to see who he recommends from his firm

Gibson, Dunn & Crutcher. It's a very specialized line of law and could quickly wind up at the Supreme Court.

"Bill has also been thinking about the medical disclosure aspect of the problem, and he asked me to think about the idea of having a panel of doctors examine Hillary's medical records and give an opinion. But he's completely opposed to releasing Hillary's medical records, and I agree. If the whole truth about her health came out, that could be fatal."

■ ■ ■

According to a guest who stayed overnight at the White House and was present in the Family Residence during a discussion of Hillary's health, Michelle Obama had a suspicion that Hillary depended on stimulant drugs to get her through the grueling campaign. The president said he had come to the same conclusion after a recent meeting with Hillary at the White House, where Hillary made an effort to persuade the Obamas to coordinate their public appearance on her behalf with Robby Mook.

"During the discussion," said the source, "Hillary suddenly broke out in a coughing fit. The president offered her a glass of water, but Hillary's coughing only grew worse. The president became so alarmed that he summoned one of the doctors on duty in the White House Medical Unit.

"While the doctor was administering to Hillary, the president, the first lady and Valerie [Jarrett] stepped outside and turned the Oval Office over to Hillary," the source continued. "After a while, the doctor emerged and told everyone that he was able to stop Hillary's convulsive coughing and that she was all right.

"But the experience left the president and first lady shaken. It was clear to them that the Hillary the public saw during the debates and rallies wasn't the same Hillary they had just seen in the Oval Office. And they concluded that there was no way she could make it through such a demanding ordeal without getting some help from booster drugs."

10

HEADED FOR TROUBLE

O n a bleak autumn day, Bill Clinton arrived in a parade of SUVs at Whitehaven, the Clintons' Georgian-style mansion in Washington, DC. He was clutching a heap of papers that contained the results of a private poll he had commissioned.

"I was with Hillary when Bill came in and waved the papers in her face," one of her friends recalled. "He said, 'This is why you are losing this goddam thing and you don't even know it. You are taking the advice of idiots and ignoring me.'

"I'd seen scenes like this before between Bill and Hillary, and this one was nothing new," the friend continued. "Hillary waved him away and laughed at him. Laughed at his rage. He was red-faced and yelling. Out of control. He said, 'You'd better fucking pay attention because it is probably already too late.' She told him he was delusional. He was the only person in the world who thought she was going to lose the election.

"He threw the papers at her feet, shook his head, and walked out the door and back to his car. Hillary slammed the door behind him."

■ ■ ■

Bill Clinton had known for some time that his wife's campaign was headed for trouble. In his view, it wasn't entirely her fault. She was a stiff and standoffish campaigner and didn't derive any joy from pumping the flesh, but she could have overcome her shortcomings and beaten a flawed candidate like Trump if she had taken his advice. Which she didn't.

"They have a very strange relationship," said someone who was close to both Clintons. "They see each other rarely. They seldom sleep in the same house. He drains her and annoys her with his constant lecturing about how she should campaign, how she should treat her team, just about everything. The reason they don't campaign together is less that he sucks the air out of the room, which he does, than the fact that he annoys her telling her what to do and always acting like the alpha dog. She has a way of tuning him out. But it saps her energy. She prefers to have conversations with him on the phone so she can hang up whenever she wants."

Bill had told Hillary that she needed to keep polling right up to Election Day, but John Podesta, her campaign chairman, and Robby Mook, her manager, said Bill was out of touch with modern mega-data collecting techniques. He didn't know what he was talking about. They painted him as an old fool.

He told Hillary that there was frustration and anger among white working class voters in the Rust Belt, which stretched from Pennsylvania to Michigan to Wisconsin. People there felt marginalized and ignored. No one in the Democratic Party seemed to feel their pain. He told her that she had to reach out to those whites, especially the men. But her campaign advisers didn't think so.

"During the campaign I traveled around the country visiting Clinton campaign offices," said one of Bill Clinton's friends, an academic who studied the techniques and methods of modern politics. "I started with the Brooklyn headquarters and talked to many at the top level as well as some unpaid interns. I went to Florida and visited a number of the dozens of offices the campaign had in that state, and I talked to many of the hundreds of workers that the campaign had hired. I went to Sandusky [Ohio] and saw the ground operation she had there. I went to Los Angeles.

"The overall impression I got of the Clinton operation was that it was chaotic," he continued. "A lot of effort was at cross purposes. Based on their mega-data, they sent a volunteer to canvass a voter, then [they sent] another and another until the voter got pissed off.

"One of the biggest problems was there were too many people giving orders, both in the field and at the highest levels of the campaign. Hillary would go around Mook and the other top people and start an operation on her own. Chelsea interfered all the time, giving orders, even firing people. Huma also interfered with the operation. It was a mess.

"Bill and his people paid no attention to Brooklyn. He wrote his own speeches and scheduled his travel without regard to the campaign organization. Many times, he acted like he was going off script like when he slammed Obamacare as the craziest thing in the world. Other times, he seemed to have lost the old Bubba magic. He contradicted Hillary and said things that couldn't be undone. Like his saying on *Charlie Rose* that she "frequently" fainted. CBS edited the version they aired to save him, but of course it got out anyway. The damage was done.

"But at bottom, Bill was right when he said that constantly attacking Trump for his defects made Hillary's staff and the media happy, but it wasn't a message that resonated with voters. Hillary came across as someone who was pissed off at her enemy [Trump], not someone who was reaching out and trying to make life better for all Americans."

11

THE UNMASKING

On October 15—three weeks before the election—attorneys from the Justice Department, the FBI, and the National Security Agency descended on the E. Barrett Prettyman Courthouse in yet another attempt to get FISA warrants against Donald Trump's campaign.

The lawyers took their places in the same courtroom as before—the Room of Requirement—but this time they faced a different circuit court judge. He had reviewed the government's previous application for warrants and found it so legally unsound that he wondered whether Attorney General Loretta Lynch had bothered to read it before she signed it. Now, as he settled into his chair, straightened his robe, and opened the court to oral arguments, he was on his guard for another muddled presentation.

However, this time the government came armed with a well-drafted application in which attorneys from the NSA presented the court with the results of extensive electronic surveillance.

Operating under Section 702 of the Foreign Intelligence Surveillance Act, the NSA monitored the emails and phone conversations between foreigners and Americans. Section 702 allowed the attorney general and the director of national intelligence to authorize spy agencies to "sweep up" the telephone and Internet data of U.S. residents who were in communication with foreign targets. However, the names of these Americans were supposed to be "minimized," or kept hidden, to protect their identity.

The NSA regularly violated those privacy protections and, without asking for permission from the FISA Court, it had "unmasked" the names of several Trump associates, including Carter Page, a foreign policy adviser, and presented the information to the new FISA Court judge.

A graduate of the United States Naval Academy, Page was the managing partner of an investment fund, Global Energy Capital. The government charged that Page, who spoke Russian, had met with Russian intelligence operatives both in New York City and Moscow, where he delivered a speech highly critical of the Obama administration's tough policy toward Russia. The government also alleged that Page had a meeting with one of Vladimir Putin's cronies, Igor Sechin, the chief executive of the energy company Rosneft.

In addition, the government charged that Page, acting as a key Trump emissary to the Kremlin, had offered the Russians a deal: if they stepped up their disinformation campaign against Hillary Clinton's campaign, Trump would reduce Washington's sanctions against Moscow after he took office.

These were grievous charges, but there were serious flaws in the government's argument.

To begin with, Carter Page wasn't a significant figure in Trump's orbit. He had never met the candidate. He had been dropped as an adviser months before. And he was willing to testify under oath that he never acted as an emissary to the Russians.

"Unfortunately for the conspiracy theorists... Carter Page was the Walter Mitty of Trump world," wrote the *Wall Street Journal's* Holman W. Jenkins Jr. "Mr. Page had been a target four years earlier of a sad little recruitment effort by the Russian spies in New York, who eventually were prosecuted and whose monitored communications referred to Mr. Page as an 'idiot.'"

Moreover, the unmasking of American names without FISA approval was a crime. Legally speaking, those names should not have been used as the basis for an FBI investigation. The unmasking also violated the Fourth Amendment to the Constitution, which protects American citizens from government intrusion in their private lives.

But somehow, the judge did not catch on to these defects in the government's application, and he granted the warrants.

The attorneys celebrated with high fives, and the FBI immediately widened its investigation of the Trump campaign. It targeted five people: Carter Page, Paul Manafort, Michael Flynn, Roger Stone, and Trump's son-in-law, Jared Kushner.

■ ■ ■

Several days after the FISA warrants were granted, the *New York Times* ran a front-page story that called into question the Trump connection to the Russian investigation. The story was datelined October 31 and ran under this headline: "Investigating Donald Trump, F.B.I. Sees No Clear Link to Russia."

"For much of the summer, the F.B.I. pursued a widening investigation into a Russian role in the American presidential campaign," the *Times* reported. "Agents scrutinized advisers close to Donald J. Trump, looked for financial connections with Russian financial figures, searched for those involved in hacking the computers of Democrats, and even chased a lead—which they ultimately came to doubt—about a possible secret channel of email communication from the Trump Organization to a Russian bank.

"Law enforcement officials say that none of the investigations so far have found any conclusive or direct link between Mr. Trump and the Russian government," the *Times* story went on. "And even the hacking into Democratic emails, the F.B.I. and intelligence officials now believe, was aimed at disrupting the presidential election rather than electing Mr. Trump."

As we shall see in future chapters, once Trump won the presidency, the editors of the *Times* did a one-eighty on the Russian story. Along with other liberal outposts, including the *Washington Post* and CNN, the *Times* unleashed an almost daily stream of "exclusive" stories—all of them based on leaks from anonymous sources—alleging that there had been a nefarious relationship between the Kremlin and Trump's associates, including his national security adviser, Michael Flynn, and his son-in-law, Jared Kushner. The relentless media onslaught would embolden Trump's enemies to talk openly of impeaching him; it would consume the attention of White House officials; it would swamp Trump's legislative agenda; and it would even threaten his hold on the presidency.

12

OCTOBER SURPRISE

I n the final days of the campaign, FBI Director James Comey sent a letter to Congress informing the lawmakers that his agents had found thousands of Huma Abedin's emails on a laptop belonging to her estranged husband, Anthony Weiner. Some of the emails had been copied from Hillary's email account and contained what appeared to be highly classified information. In light of this new information, which the FBI had yet to fully examine, Comey wrote that he was reopening the investigation of Hillary Clinton's use of her private email server.

The October surprise dominated the headlines, and Hillary immediately began bashing Comey, accusing him of a political move that could cost her the election.

"I was with Bill [Clinton] in Little Rock when he had this shouting match with Hillary on the phone and she accused Comey [of a political hit] for reviving the investigation and reversing her campaign's momentum," said one of Bill's closest advisers. "Bill didn't buy the excuse that

Comey would cost Hillary the election. As far as he was concerned, all the blame belonged to [Robby] Mook and [John] Podesta and Hillary herself because they displayed a tone-deaf attitude about the feeble economy and its impact on millions and millions of working-class voters.

"Bill was severely critical of Hillary's decision to reject an invitation to address a St. Patrick's Day event at the University of Notre Dame," the source continued. "Hillary's campaign advisers nixed the idea on the ground that white Catholics were not the audience she needed to reach.

"A big part of Bill's anger toward Hillary was that he was sidelined during the entire campaign by her advisers. He can't be effective if he sees himself as just another hired hand. He wasn't listened to and that infuriated him. After all, he knows something about campaigns, and he told me in early October that Hillary and her advisers were blowing it.

"Bill was so red in the face during the conversation that I worried he was going to have a heart attack. He got so angry that he threw the phone off the roof of his penthouse and toward the Arkansas River."

■　■　■

On November 5, three days before the election, James Comey made a stunning announcement. Since reopening the Hillary email investigation, he had found no evidence to change his original July 5 recommendation. No charges would be brought against Hillary Clinton.

His messy, inept, and incompetent handling of the investigation marked him as the Inspector Clouseau of the FBI.

13

A LONG DAY'S JOURNEY INTO NIGHT

Chelsea Clinton arrived at her mother's hotel suite with her children, Charlotte and Aiden. The kids ran over to Hillary, who was practicing her acceptance speech. Charlotte was wearing a pretty dress with an H on it—H in honor of her grandmother, who was on the verge of becoming the first woman president of the United States. Grinning from ear to ear, Hillary gave Charlotte a big hug.

Huma Abedin appeared in the art deco living room shortly after Chelsea. She was with Phillipe Reines, who had played the role of Donald Trump in Hillary's debate prep. Reines poured himself a glass of champagne and clinked glasses with John Podesta, the campaign chairman, who was so confident of victory that he had stopped doing tracking polls a couple of weeks before. Aides came and went, talking on their smart phones to colleagues at the Brooklyn campaign headquarters and in boiler rooms around the country. Everyone was giddy—everyone, that is, except Bill Clinton.

His private polling had detected ominous clouds over the Rust Belt states of Pennsylvania, Michigan, and Wisconsin. He had warned Hillary, but she had laughed at his concerns. Now he was sitting on the living room sofa with a glum expression on his face. Hillary ignored him. She drank another glass of champagne. She wasn't going to let Bill spoil the biggest night of her life.

The White House. 6:45 p.m.

A party to celebrate Hillary's victory spilled onto the White House grounds and into the Rose Garden. Some of the staff were slightly drunk, and their loud voices could be heard upstairs in the Family Quarters.

There, Barack and Michelle Obama nibbled on a buffet of chicken fingers and waffle fries. The president chatted with Valerie Jarrett as they watched the early returns on TV. He had scheduled a meeting with Hillary for November 10 to begin planning the transition.

Jarrett would later tell a friend that she had never seen the president look happier.

Javits Convention Center, New York City. 7:30 p.m.

The cannons were ready to fire shiny confetti that resembled shattered glass—a reminder of the alleged glass ceiling that until now had prevented women from reaching the White House. As early returns flashed on large TV monitors, Chuck Schumer climbed onto the stage and led the crowd in a rousing chant: "I believe she will win!"

But Chuck wasn't so sure. Exit polls in Florida and North Carolina showed that Hillary was underperforming with her key demographic, college-educated women. When Chuck checked with a Hillary aide, he was told, "Don't worry, our firewalls in Wisconsin and Michigan are strong. There's no way Trump can win."

Peninsula Hotel. 7:45 p.m.

"[Robby] Mook walked down the hall and into the Clinton suite, where he found Bill and Hillary in the living room," Jonathan Allen and Amie Parnes reported in *Shattered*, their exhaustive account of Hillary's campaign. "He stood over them—Hillary sitting in a big chair and Bill on the couch—and did his best not to sugarcoat what he was seeing in the numbers.

"'We need North Carolina, Florida, or Pennsylvania, and then we need other states,' he told them. 'Florida and North Carolina don't look great.' He stopped short of telling them that Hillary would lose Florida, but he knew that he could be looking at the front edge of [a] terrifying wave. 'We need to see if this is a Southeast problem,' he said.

"Hillary sat stone-faced, trying to process the unexpected and abrupt reversal of her fortunes. 'OK,' she said over and over as she nodded. It was all she could muster."

Trump Tower, New York City. 8:30 p.m.

Donald Trump watched the returns with his family and campaign staff in his triplex apartment. Beneath his cocksure exterior, Trump had always harbored doubts that he would win.[1] He and his campaign manager, Kellyanne Conway, had agreed on the timing of a concession phone call; they understood, even if they refused to say so, that he would likely concede to Hillary, not the other way around.

But that quickly changed. After Trump had won Florida and North Carolina and was performing well in the Rust Belt, Kellyanne's optimism began to rise.

"We kept calling him Mr. President-elect," Kellyanne said, "but he is a brilliant businessman and he knows the deal isn't consummated until everything is completed and verified and signed, sealed, and delivered."

News Corp building, New York City. 11:00 p.m.

"Hold on!" said Megyn Kelly.

"Stand by!" said Bret Baier.

"There's a big old call to make right now," said Kelly, "and that is that Fox News is projecting that Donald Trump has won the state of Wisconsin. Donald Trump has won the state of *Wisconsin*—and there goes [Hillary's] Blue Wall. That's ten electoral votes. That brings Trump up to 232, and he has officially pierced the Blue Wall that she needed to hold on to, which is momentous."

White House Residence. 11:15 p.m.

Barack Obama had a rubber ball in his hand, which he squeezed as Megyn Kelly announced the fall of Wisconsin to Trump. Obama hurled the ball across the room. It bounced off a wall and nearly knocked over a lamp.

"What the hell do we do now?" he asked.

"We call Hillary and tell her to concede," Valerie Jarrett said. "It's over. She's dead; she just doesn't know it yet."

Jarrett got in touch with David Simas, the White House political director, and instructed him to phone Robby Mook.

"What's going on in your camp?" Simas asked Mook, according to a reconstruction of their conversation by the authors of *Shattered*.

"I don't think we're going to win," Mook said.

"I don't think you are either," Simas agreed. "POTUS doesn't think it's wise to drag this out."

But Hillary wouldn't budge. Trump's margins in Michigan and Wisconsin were paper-thin. Maybe the tide would turn in her favor.

Jarrett had convinced Obama he needed to act decisively in order to avoid a messy post-election recount. He called Hillary himself.

"You need to concede," he told her.

She still wouldn't budge.

Obama then called John Podesta and gave him the same message.

Peninsula Hotel/Javits Convention Center. About 1:00 a.m. November 9, 2016

"After Pennsylvania went to Trump, Hillary and Podesta left the living room and went to another room, and I heard the sound of glass breaking," a campaign aide, who was present all night long, said in an interview for this book. "When Hillary emerged, tears were streaming down her face, smearing her makeup. Huma was with her and had a hand on Hillary's shoulder. She was crying as well.

"Podesta decided it was time to go to the Javits Center to thank the faithful," the aide continued. "I went with him in his car on the way downtown as he prepared his speech. He was talking to people on his phone about the need to get a recount in key states.

"When we got to the Center, the place was already emptying out. Podesta told those who remained that the fight was just beginning and that they shouldn't give up hope.

"As he spoke, workmen were dumping the unused shattered-ceiling confetti into green trash bags. The vast empty hall was littered with crushed Desani water bottles."

Trump Tower/Hilton Hotel. About 1:00 a.m.

Kellyanne Conway was unable to contain her joy. The Associated Press had just called Pennsylvania for Trump. She persuaded Trump and his family and campaign staff to decamp from Trump Tower and head to the Hilton Hotel, where hundreds of ecstatic Trump supporters were celebrating his victory.

Trump wondered if they should wait until Hillary conceded.

"Why don't we do there what we are doing here?" Kellyanne said to Trump. "We can stay at the [Hilton] headquarters all night or a week if we have to."

Peninsula Hotel. 2:30 a.m.

Huma Abedin phoned Kellyanne Conway at the Hilton Hotel and asked her to put Donald Trump on the phone.

Hillary took the phone from Huma. She could hear a delirious Trump crowd whooping it up in the background. According to a source who heard her side of the conversation, Hillary tried to sound like a graceful loser, but the words stuck in her throat.

"Congratulations, Donald," she barely managed to say.

PART TWO

TRANSITION

14

STATE OF DENIAL

"**H**illary Clinton's campaign blithely assumed that rallying 'people of color' and Millennials would produce victory," the *Washington Examiner's* Michael Barone wrote shortly after the election. "They didn't figure that Midwest non-college whites, who had long voted Democratic, wouldn't be dazzled by Lady Gaga concerts.

"And the Democrats' plight [was] all the more poignant because right up until election night, many of them believed that the future was forever theirs," Barone continued. "And with some reason. Ruy Teixeira and John Judis's 2002 book *The Emerging Democratic Majority*[1] pointed the way, predicting that blacks, Hispanics and single women would produce increasing Democratic margins over time. *National Journal's* Ronald Brownstein and Democratic pollster Stanley Greenberg in his 2015 book *Ascendant America* thoroughly elaborated on this theme.

"But a vulgarized version of this idea got many Democrats—apparently including the Clinton high command in Brooklyn—thinking an eternal Democratic majority was a dead certainty."

Instead, the Clintonistas came face-to-face with electoral catastrophe.

■   ■   ■

"This is a disaster!"

That's how Anna Galland, the executive director of MoveOn.org, portrayed the election of Donald Trump. "We fought our hearts out to avert this reality," Galland groused in an email she dispatched on the night of Trump's victory to the eight million members of MoveOn.org, the online progressive protest movement.[2] "We need to make it clear that we will continue to stand together."

Though most Americans have never heard of Galland, she is one of the most powerful leftwing activists in the country and one of the chief villains in the plot to destroy Trump. A thirty-seven-year-old mother of twins who lives in the college town of Ann Arbor, Michigan, Galland comes across in TV interviews as a rather harmless community organizer. But one word from Galland is all it takes to send tens of thousands of MoveOn.org members into the streets. And true to form, her call to "stand together" against Trump was met with instant, massive, and often violent demonstrations.

The worst outbreak of violence occurred in Portland, Oregon. Thousands of protesters poured onto the streets in what the police called "a riot." The protesters hurled bottles and road flares at the police, attacked a film crew, sprayed graffiti on cars and buildings, and smashed shop windows. The sound of gunfire could be heard over their chant: "We reject the president-elect!"

In Indianapolis, two police officers were injured by protesters throwing rocks. In Los Angeles, marchers burned a paper bust of Trump and blocked the city freeways. In Oakland, California, protesters threw gasoline bombs and fireworks at police and blocked highways with garbage fires. In New York City, a large group of marchers gathered outside Trump Tower, where they were joined by Lady Gaga, who stood on the back of a truck waving a sign, "Love Trumps Hate!"

The protests lasted five nights. Tens of thousands participated. Asked by reporters to explain exactly why they were so angry, many of the protesters said they couldn't accept the fact that Hillary had lost the election. It was unfair. It was too much to bear. They sounded as though they had suffered a death in the family. Hillary's shocking loss cast them into the first stages of grief—anger and denial.

■ ■ ■

No one was in greater denial than Hillary herself.

"She put a fine point on the factors she believed cost her the presidency: the FBI (Comey), the KGB (the old name for Russia's intelligence service), and the KKK (the support Trump got from white nationalists)," wrote Jonathan Allen and Amie Parnes. "Hillary declined to take responsibility for her own loss.... Mook and Podesta assembled her communications team at the Brooklyn headquarters to engineer the case that the election wasn't entirely on the up-and-up. For a couple of hours, with Shake Shack containers littering the room, they went over the script they would pitch to the press and public. Already, Russian hacking was the centerpiece of the argument."

The architects of Hillary's campaign refused to man up and take responsibility for their doomed effort. At a forum hosted by Harvard University's Kennedy School of Government, Jennifer Palmieri, Hillary's churlish communications director, attacked Kellyanne Conway, Trump's campaign manager, for running on a platform of white supremacy and catering to the "alt-right."[3] Their exchange quickly exploded into a shouting match.

> **Palmieri:** If providing a platform for white supremacists makes me a brilliant tactician, I am glad to have laws. I am more proud of Hillary Clinton's alt-right speech than any other moment on the campaign trail.
>
> **Conway:** Wow.

Palmieri: She had the courage to stand up. I would rather lose than win the way you guys did.

Conway: No you wouldn't. No you wouldn't.

Palmieri: Yes, yes.

Conway: That's very clear today. No you wouldn't. I'm sorry, how exactly did we win? How exactly did we win? I'd like to know because I sacrificed the last four months of my life to do it, excuse me, and we did it. And we did it by looking at the schedule and, yes, the electoral map of 270 because that is how you win the presidency. And we went into places where we were either ignored or mocked roundly by most of the people in this room. I have a smile on my face at all times.... We connected with voters.

Palmieri: One of my proudest moments with [Hillary] is her standing up with courage and with clarity in Steve Bannon's own words and Donald Trump's own words the platform that they gave to white supremacists.... I am very glad to be part of the campaign that tried to stop this.

Conway: Excuse me, she said white supremacists.... Do you think I ran a campaign where white supremacists had a platform? Are you going to look me in the face and tell me that?

Palmieri: It did. Kellyanne, it did.

Conway: Oh, that's how you lost?...Do you think you could have just had a decent message for the white working class voters?

■   ■   ■

Hillary spent a billion dollars on her campaign—at least four times more than Trump. She came within a hair's breadth—fewer than 100,000 votes—of winning Pennsylvania, Wisconsin, and Michigan. Her big-bucks donors—Dustin Moskovitz, co-founder of Facebook; Donald Sussman, president of Paloma Partners hedge fund; Jay Robert Pritzker, heir to the Hyatt Hotel fortune; Haim Saban, chairman of Univision; George Soros; and others—couldn't fathom how she had managed to lose an election with so much money. Didn't Joe Kennedy, JFK's father, say, "Politics is like war. It takes three things to win. The first is money and the second is money and the third is money."

Her top donors wanted a recount of the vote. And when it became clear that Hillary had won nearly three million more popular votes than Trump, the donors were joined by a coalition of liberal activists, academics, and election experts who put pressure on the Clinton campaign for a recount. Behind the scenes, John Podesta and Donna Brazile, the interim chairman of the Democratic National Committee, lobbied Hillary to challenge the official tally of votes.

Most of the pressure for a recount fell on Marc Elias, Hillary's general counsel. "Since the day after the election, we have had lawyers and data scientists and analysts combing over the results to spot anomalies that would suggest a hacked result," Elias said in an online post.

As Hillary's team dithered about the recount, Jill Stein, the Green Party presidential candidate, who had won 1 percent of the vote, stepped forward. Sensing an opportunity to raise her profile and that of her far-left party, she launched a fundraising campaign. The response was overwhelming: Stein hauled in $5 million in less than three days.

Several people close to Hillary—Huma Abedin, Chelsea Clinton, and Sidney Blumenthal—encouraged her to ask for a recount, not because they thought it would change the outcome, but because they thought it would help lift her spirits.

"She is weepy, looks ten years older and is very whiny," said one of Hillary's closest friends in an interview for this book. "She has been drinking wine pretty heavily, much more than usual. She mopes around all day, swimming in a sea of recriminations and complaining that her campaign managers were 'incompetent,' Bill and Chelsea 'didn't work hard enough,' FBI director Comey was 'in league with Trump.'"

Valerie Jarrett agreed. She told Clinton's top aides that it would be in the interest of the Democratic Party if they got involved in the recount effort and not leave it to the Green Party's Jill Stein.

"The president felt that the progressives were acting stunned and helpless and had to rise out of their stupor and show that they weren't going to take their defeat lying down," said a source close to Jarrett. "Contesting the results of the election was the best and fastest way to stir the morale and fighting spirit of the demoralized party.

"Obama felt that a recount would plant a seed with the base that the election was somehow dishonest," the source continued. "He wanted to raise serious questions about the legitimacy of the Trump presidency."

And what did Bill Clinton—the man Charlie Rose once called "the best political animal that's ever been in American politics"—think of the recount talk?

Said a close Clinton adviser: "Bill thinks the recount is going to back-fire as a strategy because there are probably no more than a handful of questionable ballots and they could actually wind up adding to Trump's numbers and validate rather than invalidate his election."

Under mounting pressure from all sides, Hillary finally agreed to back the Wisconsin recount effort. Her general counsel, Marc Elias, explained that while there was no evidence of Russian sabotage of the vote tally, the campaign felt "an obligation to the more than 64 million Americans who cast their ballots for Hillary Clinton. We certainly understand the heartbreak felt by so many who worked so hard to elect Hillary Clinton."

In other words, the Clinton campaign favored a recount in order to make Hillary's supporters feel good.

In the end, it didn't make any difference. The final Wisconsin tally actually strengthened Trump's hand. He increased his margin of victory in that state by 131 votes, leaving him more than 22,000 votes ahead of Hillary. Federal courts blocked the recount in Pennsylvania and Michigan. But before the court order went into effect in Michigan, the state did a partial recount. The results gave Hillary an additional 102 votes.

■ ■ ■

Next, Democratic activists turned their attention to the Electoral College. Two hundred and seventy were needed to win; Trump had 306.

Could he be stopped?

In fifty-six nationwide elections over the course of more than two centuries, the winner of the Electoral College had never been denied the presidency. Many Democrats thought it was time to ignore that precedent, and they appealed directly to two members of Hillary's team—senior adviser Jake Sullivan and communications director Jennifer Palmieri—to help them convince their candidate.

"Call logs, emails and text messages reveal a Clinton campaign walking a tightrope—never fully endorsing the effort [to block Trump's electoral vote], but intentionally declining to stamp it out," wrote *Politico's* Kyle Cheney. "The approach was comparable, one former campaign official said, to the campaign's passive-but-not-dismissive response to long-shot recounts in Wisconsin, Michigan and Pennsylvania. Indeed, as news of Russia's role in influencing the election emerged, an exhausted and shell-shocked Clinton team at times appeared torn between accepting the election results and continuing to publicly fight Trump's ascension to the White House."

The goal was simple, if dubious. Using ads, phone calls, texts, emails, and in-your-face action, the activists would try to coax or cajole thirty-seven of the 306 Republican electors who were pledged to Trump to vote for some other Republican—say, Ohio Governor John Kasich or 2012 GOP nominee Mitt Romney. That would leave Trump with 269 votes—one short of victory—and throw the election into the House of Representatives.

The House was controlled by Republicans, but the Democrats who were behind the effort to stop Trump—they called themselves the Hamilton Electors—were hoping that enough Trump-haters in the House would vote for a different Republican.

On December 12—seven days before the electors were scheduled to vote in their respective states—the U.S. intelligence community issued a report concluding that Russia had meddled in the election. Hillary's campaign chairman, John Podesta, who was consumed by bitterness over his loss, seized the opportunity to demand that the members of the Electoral College receive an intelligence briefing in the hopes that it would influence their vote against Trump.

"Electors have a solemn responsibility under the Constitution and we support their efforts to have their questions addressed," Podesta said.

"It is...worth noting the extraordinary lengths that Democrats and the progressive media have gone to attempt to lobby electors to vote for Hillary Clinton or a Republican alternative," the *Wall Street Journal* editorialized. " 'Electors under siege,' said a headline in *Politico*, reporting that many 'have been inundated by harassing phone calls and hate mail,' even 'death threats.' So much for the calm deliberation that progressives claim to want as they lobbied electors under the rubric of Hamilton's Electors. The spectacle of the last month has been an exercise in political intimidation, precisely the kind of pressure politics that Alexander Hamilton wanted an Electoral College to protect the country *from*."

On Sunday, December 19, protesters, who had been organized by MoveOn.org's Anna Galland, descended on the Wisconsin electors as they assembled to vote.

"You sold out our country," screamed a woman. "Every one of you, you're pathetic. You don't deserve to be in America."

The crowd chanted: "Shame, shame, shame."

Afterward, Galland crowed that the protest was "a marker for what's to come."

But like the recount effort, the campaign to suborn the electors flopped. Only two Republicans—both in Texas—ignored their legal duty and voted against Trump.

"The professional political left is attempting to foment a permanent opposition that is corrosive to our constitutional democracy, and ignores what just happened in this election," Kellyanne Conway said. "[Liberals cannot] wave magic pixie dust and make this go away."

It was not for a lack of trying.

15

OPEN SEASON ON TRUMP

"The country is in the throes of a major epidemic, with no known cure and some pretty scary symptoms," wrote Justin Raimondo, a contributing editor at *The American Conservative*. "It's called Trump Derangement Syndrome.

"In the first stage of the disease," Raimondo went on, "victims lose all sense of proportion.... In the advanced stages of the disease, the afflicted lose touch with reality. Opinion is unmoored from fact."

Nowhere was the disease more virulent than in the worlds of popular music and movies. During the campaign, Hillary Clinton raised ten times more money than Donald Trump in Hollywood. She was fêted by the town's royalty, and was elevated to the status of near-sainthood.

The movie and music industries haven't always been a bastion of liberalism. In the Golden Era of Hollywood, many movie moguls and stars were conservative Republicans, including Cecil B. DeMille, Louis B. Mayer, Samuel Goldwyn, Walt Disney, Gary Cooper, Jimmy Stewart, Clark Gable, John Wayne, Bing Crosby, Mickey Rooney, Shirley Temple, Robert Mitchum, William Holden, Steve McQueen, Rock Hudson, George Murphy, Ronald Reagan, Dean Martin, Frank Sinatra, Charlton Heston, and Clint Eastwood, among many others. But by the 1970s, liberals were dominating the industry and driving conservatives out. Today, progressive politics has become a virtual religion in La-la Land.

"This isn't a night-life city anymore," a longtime Hollywood denizen told a writer for *National Review*. "You're expected to attend breakfast meetings [of progressive activists]. You're not up late partying. And politics fills that role. You go to fundraisers and dinners. It has become central to how you live here now."

After Trump won the election, a howl went up from Beverly Hills to Malibu. Movie stars and musicians vied with each other to prove their political piousness. It was hard to tell who was the most demented.

Robert DeNiro, the star of *Raging Bull*, ranted about Trump in a *Vice Exclusives* video. "I mean he is so blatantly stupid," said DeNiro. "He's a punk, a dog, he's a pig. Colin Powell said it best: he's a national disaster. He's an embarrassment to this country. It makes me so angry this country has gotten to this point that this fool, this bozo, has wound up where he has. He talks how he'd like to punch people in the face?... Well, I'd like to punch him in the face."

There was, of course, the obligatory comparison of Trump to Hitler. Russell Simmons, the music producer who had known and worked with Trump for many years, wrote the president-elect an open letter. "My friends, both Muslims and Jews, are saying there are so many comparisons between your rap and Hitler's," wrote Simmons, "and I cannot disagree with them, Donald."

Shock rocker Marilyn Manson, an emblem of modern decadence, released a music video in which he stood over the decapitated body of a man who resembled Trump.

In an interview with *Entertainment Weekly*, Jennifer Lawrence, who often seemed to have trouble finishing a sentence without several four-letter words, said, "If Donald Trump is president of the United States, it will be the end of the world."

Lea DeLaria, an actress on the TV series *Orange Is the New Black*, used social media to tell her followers how she'd like to deal with Trump. "Pick up a baseball bat and take out every fucking Republican and independent I see." She added the hashtags "#fucktrump," "#fuckthe GOP," "fuckstraightwhiteamerica," and "#fuckyourprivilege."

In an interview with the *Guardian*, George Clooney—who once chided a discourteous reporter for calling the president "Obama" instead of "*Mr.* Obama"—called Trump "a xenophobic fascist." When Clooney received an award in France in February 2017, he slammed America's new president, associating him with "fear" and "hate."

Arnold Schwarzenegger, who had fathered a son with his housekeeper, and been accused of sexual harassment in the past, said with a straight face that he wouldn't vote for Trump because of Trump's mistreatment of women.

Rihanna, who released a video with the warning "Language. Nudity. Violence," tweeted: "Disgusted!"

Screenwriter Aaron Sorkin (*The Social Network*), who was arrested in 2001 when guards at a security checkpoint at the Burbank Airport found hallucinogenic mushrooms, marijuana, and crack cocaine in his carry-on bag, wrote a letter to his fifteen-year-old daughter Roxy and her mother Julia Sorkin, which was published in *Vanity Fair*.

"Well the world changed last night in a way I couldn't protect us from," Sorkin began. "That's a terrible feeling for a father. I won't sugarcoat it—this is truly horrible. It's hardly the first time my candidate didn't win (in fact it's the sixth time) but it is the first time that a thoroughly incompetent pig with dangerous ideas, a serious psychiatric disorder, no knowledge of the world and curiosity to learn has.

"So what do we do?" Sorkin continued. "Here's what we'll do…we'll fucking fight. (Roxy, there's a time for this kind of language and it's now.) We're not powerless and we're not voiceless.

"Roxy, I know my predictions have let you down in the past, but personally, I don't think this guy can make it a year without committing an impeachable crime."

Kathy Griffin urged her fellow comedians to go all out on "President Piece of Shit." And she vowed to "deliver a beat down to Donald Trump and also to Barron," his eleven-year-old son.

Months after threatening the president's son (without a peep of disapproval from anyone in Hollywood), Griffin finally went too far even for the deranged Left. She posted a gruesome video on Instagram showing her holding a bloody severed head of President Trump. The stunt got her fired from her gig on CNN's New Year's Eve program, which she had hosted with Anderson Cooper since 2007.

An unrepentant Griffin then held a teary press conference in which she made a half-hearted apology—"I went way too far"—and then complained, "A sitting president of the United States and his grown children and the first lady are personally trying to ruin my life forever. You guys know [Trump], he's not going to stop. I don't think I'll have a career after this. I'm going to be honest, he broke me."

"Imagine," wrote the *New York Post*'s John Podhoretz, "living in a bubble so impermeable it didn't occur to you that retailing a photograph of a decapitated president's head would be a horrendous career move—a bubble in which you don't know anyone who doesn't think the world would be a better place once Donald Trump had had his head cut off. That is the world Kathy Griffin lives in."

And that is the world of Hollywood liberals.

16

FOLLOW THE MONEY

" **A** fierce resistance is rising to confront and constrain the Trump presidency," noted *Rolling Stone*. "From the ACLU to the Sierra Club to Everytown for Gun Safety, civil society is girding for battle—reinforced by an unprecedented upswelling of activist support and donations."

The upswelling—or the "resistance" as it came to be called—traced its financial origins to a secret three-day meeting that took place at the Mandarin Oriental Hotel in Washington, DC, the week after Trump's stunning victory. Organized by George Soros, the billionaire currency speculator, the meeting brought together three of the wealthiest progressive donor groups in America—the Women Donors Network, the Solidaire Network, and the Democracy Alliance, the largest liberal dark money organization in the country.

Many mega-rich liberal Democrats, including the environmentalist Tom Steyer and the philanthropist Donald Sussman, helped fund the

Democracy Alliance. Since the Democracy Alliance was founded in 2005, these donors had given more than $500 million to far-left organizations like Black Lives Matter and the immigrant group United We Dream. But no one had devoted as much money to Democratic candidates and liberal causes as George Soros, who contributed tens of billions of dollars.

The son of a prominent Hungarian lawyer of Jewish descent, George Soros grew up in Budapest during the Nazi occupation. His father bribed a government official to adopt György (George's Hungarian name) and pretend that the boy was his Christian godson. After Adolf Eichmann arrived in Hungary to carry out the Final Solution, György's "godfather" was placed in charge of confiscating Jewish property, and he took György with him on his house-to-house rounds.

In 1998, *60 Minutes'* Steve Kroft asked Soros if he felt any remorse or survivor's guilt about his participation in such evil.

> **Kroft:** You watched lots of people get shipped off to the death camps.
> **Soros:** Right. I was 14 years old. And I would say that that's when my character was made.
> **Kroft:** In what way?
> **Soros:** That one should think ahead. One should understand and—and anticipate events and when—when one is threatened. It was a tremendous threat of evil. I mean, it was a—a very personal experience of evil.
> **Kroft:** I mean, that's—that sounds like an experience that would send lots of people to the psychiatric couch for many, many years. Was it difficult?
> **Soros:** Not—not at all. Not at all. Maybe as a child you don't—you don't see the connection. But it was—it created no—no problem at all.
> **Kroft:** No feeling of guilt?
> **Soros:** No.

Those who knew Soros said that his experience during the Holocaust left him with delusions of grandeur—what some would call a messiah complex.

Soros didn't disagree.

"I fancied myself as some kind of god," he once wrote. "If truth be known, I carried some rather potent messianic fantasies with me from childhood, which I felt I had to confront, otherwise they might get me in trouble."

Another time, he told Britain's *Independent* newspaper: "It is a sort of disease when you consider yourself some kind of god, the creator of everything, but I feel comfortable about it now since I began to live it out."

Soros lived out his dreams by accumulating great wealth and power. He was known as "The Man Who Broke the Bank of England" because of his short sale of $10 billion worth of pound sterling during the UK currency crisis in 1992. The windfall from that one sale netted him $1 billion and set him on the road to unimaginable riches. Nothing seemed to stop him, not even a 2002 conviction in France for insider trading. By 2016, he was worth $25.2 billion, which made him one of the twenty-nine richest people in the world.

Despite his wealth, Soros was still as eager as ever to confiscate other peoples' property and money. He believed he was on a mission to save America from the "evil" influences of free market capitalism.

The thrice-married eighty-six-year-old Soros (his current wife, Tamiko Bolton, is forty-two years his junior) put his money behind a host of far-left causes: confiscatory taxes of the rich, abortion, physician-assisted suicide, legalized marijuana, unrestricted immigration, government funded media, and a greatly reduced American involvement in the world.

"[His] global reach and influence far outstrip those of the Koch brothers or other liberal bogeymen," Stefan Kanfer wrote in *City Journal*. "Underlying it all is a vision both dystopian and opportunistic. 'The main obstacle to a stable and just world order,' Soros has declared, 'is the United States.' Ergo, that constitutional republic must be weakened and its allies degraded. The Sorosian world order—one of open borders and global governance, antithetical to the ideals and experience of the West—could then assume command."

■ ■ ■

Soros rarely attended meetings of the Democracy Alliance, but after the shocking Trump victory, he made an exception and delivered a speech at the secret gathering that launched the resistance.

The press was barred from the meeting, and the participants were forbidden to discuss the proceedings, but the identity of some of the attendees leaked out. They included House Democratic leader Nancy Pelosi; Senator Elizabeth Warren of Massachusetts; Representative Keith Ellison of Minnesota; Neera Tanden of the Center for American Progress; Denise Feriozzi, political director of the pro-abortion group EMILY'S List; Heather Hargreaves, vice president of NextGen Climate; and dozens of super-rich Democracy Alliance "Partners."[1]

Soros presented a plan to merge the three major donor groups— the Women Donors Network, the Solidaire Network, and the Democracy Alliance—into a powerful new fund specifically aimed at undermining Donald Trump's agenda and developing a rapid response to Republican policies. He called it the Emergent Fund and assigned it the task of fighting "threats" to immigrants, women, Muslims, African Americans, and LGBTQ communities.

Soros asked Senator Warren to deliver the keynote address, and according to those who heard her speech, Warren lambasted the Democratic Party for losing its touch with the common man and woman. It was time for revolutionary change.

"The DA [Democracy Alliance], its donors and beneficiary groups over the last decade have had a major hand in shaping the institutions of the left, including orienting some of its key organizations around Clinton, and by basing their strategy around the idea that minorities and women constituted a so-called 'rising American electorate' that could tip elections to Democrats," wrote Kenneth Vogel, the chief investigative reporter of *Politico*.

"That didn't happen in the presidential election, where Trump won largely on the strength of his support from working-class whites," Vogel continued. "Additionally, exit polls suggested that issues like fighting climate change and the role of money in politics—which the DA's beneficiary groups have used to try to turn out voters—didn't resonate as much with the voters who carried Trump to victory."

"'The DA itself should be called into question,' said one Democratic strategist who has been active in the group and [attended] the meeting. 'You can make a very good case it's nothing more than a social club for a handful of wealthy white donors and labor union officials to drink wine and read memos, as the Democratic Party burns down around them.'"

17

THE RISE OF THE RESISTANCE

"**I** joined the resistance because I wanted to shape the world the way I wanted it shaped, not the way Trump wanted it shaped," Lori Koons, a sixty-something San Francisco beauty salon owner, said in an interview for this book. "I've been donating money, raising money, signing petitions, and organizing the opposition. There are over a million members in California alone of the Courage Campaign. We meet in small groups in peoples' homes, at my salon, wherever we can to brainstorm ideas for the resistance."

Lori Koons was typical of the hundreds of thousands of Democratic activists—many of them Bernie Sanders supporters—who made up what the *Washington Post* called "a restive, active and aggressive base." Most of the people in this base lived on the East or West coast and resided in sanctuary cities that sheltered illegal immigrants.[1] These urban dwellers could choose from scores of liberal protest groups, including such Soros-funded organizations as the Center for American Progress, MoveOn.org, the Working Families Party, Occupy Wall Street, the Black Lives Matter Network, and United We Dream (an immigrant youth organization).

The most effective project to emerge in the early days of the resistance movement was called Indivisible. A twenty-six-page step-by-step online guide for activists, it was launched by a group of two dozen current and former congressional staffers, including the husband-and-wife team of Ezra Levin and Leah Greenberg.

"We were going through the stages of grief, like a lot of progressives," Levin explained, "and wanted to do what we could to help."

"When we put it online," said Greenberg, "we thought that our friends were going to read it, and they would go home to families at Christmas and somebody would say, 'What can I do?', and our friends would give them that Google doc, and in six months somebody would email us and they'd say, 'Hey, I used your guide at a town hall,' and we would be really excited."

Indivisible was based on the confrontational tactics perfected by Saul Alinsky, the community activist who had greatly influenced the thinking of Barack Obama and Hillary Clinton. Indivisible targeted members of Congress with rowdy town halls, visits to their district offices, and a flood of calls on their Washington phone lines.

"Grab seats at the front of the room [at Republican town halls] but do not all sit together," the Indivisible guide advised protesters. "This will help reinforce the impression of broad consensus. [Ask] hostile questions [and keep] a firm hold on the mic."

The chaotic results—screaming, disorderly town hall meetings that were designed to shame Republican lawmakers—resembled the fanatical Red Guards' disruptions during China's Cultural Revolution. Many of the protests were caught on iPhone cameras and broadcast on the nightly TV news shows, leaving the impression that the resistance was more pervasive than it actually was.

"Every member of Congress cares about how their constituents view them and the narrative being formed in their districts," said Sarah Dohl, one of the contributors to the Indivisible guide. "And we're not just focused on Republicans. This is about Democrats standing up and having a spine and pushing back against Trump and Republicans."

The Indivisible guide went viral as soon as it was posted. George Takei, who starred in the television series *Star Trek*, tweeted it out to his 2.2 million followers. Former Clinton administration Labor Secretary Robert Reich followed with a mass tweet of his own.

"We just had no idea it would turn into this huge movement," said Dohl, who seemed amazed that Indivisible had registered 6,200 affiliate chapters on its website and been downloaded more than 1.7 million times.

Indivisible did not disclose its donors, which raised the obvious question: where did it get its funding?

"It doesn't matter who we take money from—we're always going to get blamed as a Soros group, even if we don't take money from Soros," said Angel Padilla, a co-founder of the group.

Padilla's attitude toward money was disingenuous. Money was the mother's milk of the resistance, and like so many leaders of the movement, Padilla himself was a member of a group—the National Immigration Law Center—that was financed by George Soros' Open Society Foundations.

Liberals like Padilla were fond of pointing out that the vast majority of people who appeared at rallies or engaged in other protest activities did so spontaneously, and that they did not receive money for showing up. But what Padilla and others conveniently overlooked was that the protests were bolstered by union organizers and paid professional agitators. It took money to bus hundreds of protesters to a site, furnish them with ready-made placards, feed them, and then bus them back home.

Like most of the other resistance groups, Indivisible could not have functioned on its own. It received organizational assistance and funding from well-heeled progressive groups such as Anna Galland's MoveOn. org, Organizing for Action (a spinoff from Barack Obama's first presidential campaign), Soros' Open Society Foundations, and the American Civil Liberties Union.[2]

Asked on *Fox and Friends* whether "people were being paid to protest," White House press secretary Sean Spicer put it this way: "Protesting has become a profession now. They have every right to do that, don't get me wrong. But I think we need to call it what it is. It's not these organic uprisings that we have seen over the last several decades. The Tea Party was a very organic movement. This has become a very paid, Astroturf-type movement."

18

OBAMA TURNS ON TRUMP

T wo days after the election, Barack Obama invited Donald Trump to the White House. He was Mr. Charm himself. He gave Trump a tour of the Oval Office, briefed him on the biggest threat to national security (North Korea's nuclear program), urged him not to hire General Michael Flynn as his national security adviser (Obama despised the obstreperous Flynn and had fired him from his job as director of the Defense Intelligence Agency), promised a smooth transition, and posed with Trump for the TV cameras.

While the men were talking, Michelle Obama was upstairs in the Family Quarters having tea with Melania Trump. The official White House photographer snapped a picture of the women sitting side by side and engaged in animated conversation. When the photo was released to the press, it generated almost as much attention as the videotaped Oval Office get-together between the president and the president-elect.

The image that Obama projected in the media was that of a president who wasn't the least bit rattled by the outcome of the election. But a source close to the Obama family with whom I spoke portrayed a far different picture. He described an angry, deeply hurt, and depressed Obama, who couldn't get over his party's defeat at the polls, which he took as a personal repudiation by the American people.

"The Obama White House is the grimmest place in the world," the source told me. "The atmosphere is funereal: everybody looks like they just lost their best friend and dog. Barack is supposed to be cheering people up, but he can barely muster a smile. He knows there's nothing he can do to make his staff feel any better. He says his whole staff needs counseling to get over their grief.

"Valerie [Jarrett] says that Barack is the worst she's ever seen him," the source continued. "He's grumpy and snaps at people. Michelle is even worse; she's enraged. Valerie says she's tried to keep the Obamas separated during the work day, because they bring each other down even more.

"Everybody believes that once it's over and the Obamas move into their new house in DC, things will be better. But as long as they're in the White House, it's a constant reminder that Donald Trump is preparing to move in and replace them."

■   ■   ■

Nine days after the election, Admiral Mike Rogers, the director of the National Security Agency, traveled to New York City to meet with Trump in Trump Tower. Vice President Mike Pence, the chairman of Trump's transition team, was considering Rogers as a potential pick for director of national intelligence, the chief intel spook. The trip, which Rogers failed to report to his bosses in the military chain of command, later raised questions in intelligence circles about why he had kept the trip a secret and what he told Trump during his interview.[1]

In his eagerness to land the top job, did Rogers tip off Trump that the FBI was investigating allegations that members of his campaign had colluded with the Russians? Did he tell Trump that the FBI was collecting information on several of Trump's closest associates?

Rogers never answered those questions, but in the weeks following his trip to New York, the media was awash with leaks from the FBI and other branches of the intelligence community about the Russian investigation. These stories—all based on illegal leaks from anonymous sources and many that turned out to be untrue—buttressed Hillary's claim that she had been robbed of victory. They dominated the news and stoked the resistance.[2]

Despite Obama's post-election promise to give Trump the chance to launch his presidential agenda "without somebody popping off in every instance," he soon changed his mind. Through surrogates like David Axelrod and David Plouffe—the political strategists who had engineered his two election victories—Obama encouraged the leaders of the resistance to exploit the Russian collusion story and undermine Trump's claim to legitimacy.

"Mr. Trump obviously knew that Russia was engaged in malicious cyber activity that was helping him and hurting Secretary Clinton's campaign," White House press secretary Josh Earnest told a press conference. "First of all it is just a fact—and you have it all on tape—that the Republican nominee for president was encouraging Russia to hack his opponent because he believed that that would help his campaign. That's not a controversial statement. I'm not trying to be argumentative, but I am trying to acknowledge a basic fact. And all of you saw it. This is not in dispute."

Earnest's comment drew an immediate response from Kellyanne Conway, who had been Trump's campaign manager and stayed on as a senior adviser.

"That is incredibly disappointing to hear from the podium of the White House press secretary," she said. "Because he basically—he essentially stated that the president-elect had knowledge of this, maybe even fanned the flames. It's incredibly irresponsible, and I wonder if his boss, President Obama, agrees."

He did.

In fact, the moment of kumbaya between Obama and Trump had vanished and an atmosphere of tension and mutual suspicion took its place. Obama went so far as to claim that if he had been the candidate instead of Hillary, he would have easily beaten Trump, and the Democrats would have maintained control of the White House.

"I am confident in this vision because I'm confident that if I had run again and articulated it, I think I could've mobilized a majority of the American people to rally behind it," Obama told David Axelrod in an interview on "The Axe Files" podcast.

That jab provoked a counterpunch from Trump, who tweeted: "President Obama said that he thinks he would have won against me. He should say that but I say NO WAY!—jobs leaving, ISIS, OCare, etc."

The media picked up the signals that the transition wasn't going as smoothly as touted.

"President Obama is dishing out a much rockier transfer of power to Donald Trump than he received from his predecessor eight years ago," wrote the *Washington Times*' Dave Boyer, "from accusing the president-elect of being aided by Russian hackers to first lady Michelle Obama's complaint that the nation has lost hope."

As usual, the first lady didn't mince words.

"I think we feel the difference now," Michelle told Oprah Winfrey in an interview that was broadcast on CBS. "See, now we're feeling what not having hope feels like. Hope is necessary. It's a necessary concept. What else do you have, if you don't have hope? What do you give your kids if you can't give them hope?"[3]

■ ■ ■

Upon returning from his annual Christmas vacation in Hawaii, Obama set up several roadblocks to Trump's presidential agenda.

One of his first steps was to endorse a decision by Donna Brazile, the interim chairman of the Democratic National Committee, to create a war room to battle the incoming president. To lead the effort, Brazile hired John Neffinger, a longtime Democratic operative, and several veterans of Hillary Clinton's campaign, including Zac Petkanas, Clinton's rapid-response director, Adrienne Watson, a campaign spokeswoman, and Tessa Simonds, an expert on digital organizing.

The war room was essentially an extension of the shady empire created by David Brock, Hillary's reich minister of propaganda, who founded Media Matters, American Bridge, and the laughably named Citizens for Responsibility and Ethics in Washington. Even dyed-in-the-wool Democrats like Neera Tanden, head of the Center for American Progress, couldn't stand the slimy Brock. She called him a "menace." John Podesta dubbed him an "unhinged narcissist."

"The new hires…have roots in the various political organizations founded by David Brock," wrote the *Washington Post's* Philip Rucker. "Neffinger has been president of the Franklin Forum, where he trained scores of Democratic candidates on communications strategy and television presentation skills. He helped coach the podium speakers at the 2016 Democratic National Convention. Petkanas and Watson have more traditional campaign experience. Before joining the Clinton campaign, Petkanas served as vice president of Media Matters for America, and before that as communications director for former Senate Democratic leader Harry M. Reid…. Before going to work for Clinton's campaign, Watson was communications director for Correct the Record, a pro-Clinton super PAC founded by Brock."

On January 12, 2017, Obama took an even more drastic step; he ordered James Clapper, the director of national intelligence, to lower the classification level of secret intelligence documents. Clapper gladly complied. This allowed the wide dissemination throughout the intelligence community of the unmasked names of Trump's campaign aides, who were suspected of dealing with the Russians.

Just as Susan Rice had hoped, the unmasked names were picked up by anti-Trump members of the Deep State and leaked to the press. On January 19, a *New York Times* story revealed that three of Trump's advisers—Paul Manafort, Carter Page, and Roger Stone—were the subject of the FBI counterintelligence investigation. The *Times* based its account on a "half-dozen current and former officials." Susan Rice's plan to sabotage President-elect Trump before he had a chance to assume office and get his presidency off the ground was in full swing.

"With less than three weeks before the Obama White House is history, making way for a new administration with radically different priorities, the president is using every power at his disposal to cement his legacy and establish his priorities as the law of the land," wrote the *New York Times*' Michael D. Shear. "He has banned oil drilling off the Atlantic coast, established new environmental monuments, protected funding for Planned Parenthood clinics, ordered the transfer of detainees from Guantanamo Bay [and] criticized Israeli settlements."

Israel turned out to be a flashpoint between Obama and Trump. Obama announced that he was considering abandoning decades of U.S. policy toward Israel. For years, America had vetoed UN Security Council resolutions condemning Israeli settlement building. The next time around, the White House said, America might abstain and let the Security Council vote go through.

In response, Israel's Prime Minister Benjamin "Bibi" Netanyahu asked Trump to apply pressure on the Obama administration before it was too late. Trump eagerly complied with Bibi's request; he tweeted messages of support for Israel and accused Obama of damaging relations with America's most important ally in the Middle East.

"Stay strong," Trump advised Israel. And he assured the Israelis that he would look out for them after he took office.

"President-elect Trump," Bibi tweeted back, "thank you for your warm friendship and your clear-cut support for Israel!"

Ten days before the Security Council vote, Ben Rhodes, the deputy director of the National Security Council, accused Israel of colluding with Trump against the sitting president.

"You're breaching tradition!" Rhodes yelled at Ron Dermer, Israel's ambassador to Washington.

"No," said Dermer, "the United States' vote is breaching tradition."

"The outgoing Obama administration lied to Trump that they hadn't made a decision whether to veto the resolution when in fact they had cooked up the whole UN thing behind the scenes," said a diplomat who was familiar with the altercation. "They never hesitated. When the vote came up, they abstained."

The lack of cooperation between the White House and the Trump transition team became even more acute when Obama placed new sanctions on Russia and expelled thirty-five Russian diplomats in retaliation for the Kremlin's interference in the American election. Trump learned about the expulsion of the Russian diplomats from TV newscasts.

"Susan Rice should have called [General Michael] Flynn [who was in line to become Trump's national security adviser] and told him that the White House was going to sanction Russia," said the diplomat. "But she didn't inform him. So Flynn reached out to the Russian ambassador on the same day Obama expelled the Russian diplomats and told Kislyak, 'We weren't aware of this, and we want to cooperate with you, so don't retaliate by expelling Americans from Moscow.' I don't see anything wrong with that.[4]

"The relationship between the Obama White House and the Trump transition people became highly contentious," the diplomat continued. "From the White House's perspective, Trump was going to destroy Obama's greatest foreign achievement, the Iran nuclear deal. Ben Rhodes, who was instrumental in putting that deal together, told me, 'The Trumps will destroy our entire legacy. It's all going to be reduced to ashes.'"

That, it turned out, was the one thing Donald Trump and Barack Obama agreed on.

19

FAKE NEWS

A key document in the plot to destroy Trump was a dossier compiled on behalf of his enemies by a former MI6 British intelligence officer named Christopher Steele. [1]

Steele was hired by Fusion GPS, an opposition-research outfit that dug up dirt on political targets. The co-founder of Fusion GPS was Glenn Simpson, a former *Wall Street Journal* reporter who was known to be buddy-buddy with Democrats. The dossier contained sensational charges that the Russian Federal Security Service had *kompromat*, or compromising information, on Trump that could be used to blackmail him. According to Steele's dossier, Trump had sex with Russian prostitutes when he visited Moscow, and had encouraged the prostitutes to give each other a "golden shower," a humiliating sex act in which one partner urinates on the other.

Fusion GPS' Glenn Simpson refused to reveal who paid for the British dossier, although it was widely reported that a Democrat donor had helped finance Christopher Steele's dirty work, and that the donor might have been working on behalf of Hillary Clinton and her campaign.

To many experienced intelligence professionals, the dossier read like typical Russian disinformation spread by its intelligence services against presumed enemies. If, as seemed likely, the Democrats and Fusion GPS worked hand in glove with the Russians, the political implications were enormous. It blew a hole in the media's favorite Russian conspiracy theory. For it would mean that it was the Clinton campaign, not the Trump campaign, that had colluded with the Russians.

Most of the charges in the dossier, including that Trump had associated with prostitutes in Moscow, were based on Steele's interviews with anonymous "Russian sources," and turned out to be false. Though experts dismissed the dossier as fake news, CNN's Wolf Blitzer picked up the dossier story and, with the assistance of CNN contributor Carl Bernstein, gave the story the kind of credibility it did not deserve.[2]

"We could not corroborate the sourcing [of the dossier]," admitted James Clapper, the director of national intelligence under President Obama.[3]

Nonetheless, the villains used the dossier as a tool to smear Trump and undermine his presidency. And the media played along. Here is how the story unfolded in the press:

■ ■ ■

John McCain passes dossier alleging secret Trump-Russia contacts to FBI:
Russian intelligence alleged to have compromising material on Trump
By Julian Borger, the *Guardian*

Senator John McCain passed documents to the FBI director, James Comey, [in December] alleging secret contacts between the Trump campaign and Moscow and that Russian intelligence had personally compromising material on the president-elect himself.

The *Guardian* can confirm that the dossier reached the top of the FBI by December. Senator John McCain, who was informed about the existence of the documents separately by an intermediary from a Western allied state, dispatched an emissary overseas to meet the source and then decided to present the material to Comey in a one-on-one meeting on December 9, according to a source aware of the meeting. The documents, which were first reported on last year by *Mother Jones*, are also in the hands of officials in the White House.

McCain was reluctant to get involved, according to a colleague, for fear the issue would be dismissed as a personal grudge against Trump. He pushed instead for the creation of a special Senate committee to look into connections between campaign staff and Moscow, but the proposal was blocked by the Republican leadership.

■ ■ ■

How Did Trump and Comey End Up Talking About 'Hookers' in Russia?
By Alice Ollstein, Talking Points Memo

Comey briefed President-elect Trump about the dossier in a Jan. 6 meeting at Trump Tower. The dossier, whose reliability is still the subject of considerable debate, was compiled by a retired British intelligence officer. Comey brought it to Trump's attention after Comey learned that *Buzz Feed* intended to publish the document.

■ ■ ■

@realDonaldTrump

FAKE NEWS—A TOTAL POLITICAL WITCH HUNT!

8:19 PM—10 Jan 2017

■ ■ ■

These Reports Allege Trump Has Deep Ties to Russia
By Ken Bensinger (*BuzzFeed* News Reporter), Miriam Elder (*BuzzFeed* News World Editor), and Mark Schoofs (*BuzzFeed* News Investigations Editor)

A dossier making explosive—but unverified—allegations that the Russian government has been "cultivating, supporting and assisting" President-elect Donald Trump for years and gained compromising information about him has been circulating among elected officials, intelligence agents, and journalists for weeks. CNN reported on Tuesday that a two-page synopsis of the report was given to President Obama and Trump [by James Comey].

■ ■ ■

CNN, The 'Trump Dossier' and 'Fake News'
By Scott Ritter, CNN contributor

The White House Press Secretary, Sean Spicer, when asked for a comment on the CNN [dossier] story, was dismissive of the report. "We continue to be disgusted by CNN's fake news reporting," Spicer declared. Spicer and the White House had every reason to be frustrated by the CNN report, which lacked any specificity to back up the conclusions reached.

....CNN chose instead to breathe life into a discredited dossier whose very existence screams partisan politics. It is one thing to report on the nuts and bolts of a story about the politicization of intelligence. Deliberately using CNN's journalistic cachet to give credence to highly politicized intelligence that everyone in the informational chain of custody—including the journalists involved—knew (or should have known) was factually unsustainable, is something else altogether.

That is the very definition of "fake news," and in this case, at least, CNN is guilty as charged.

20

"A NATIONWIDE ORGY OF RAGE AND SPITE"

A s the inauguration of Donald Trump neared, a disconsolate Hillary Clinton invited five of her oldest friends to Chappaqua.

"All of us were aware that it wasn't going to be pleasant to be around her," recalled a woman who was part of the group. "But she wanted a pity party, so we showed up with bottles of her favorite Coppola Chardonnay and sinful amounts of Godiva chocolate.

"I've known her for almost fifty years, and the election loss was the worst thing that's ever happened to her," the friend continued. "It pitched her into a state of black despair, and it seemed she'd never recover. She stayed holed up at Chappaqua, because the last place in the world she wanted to be was Washington.

"She was drinking too much wine, which tends to make her belligerent and sadder rather than happier. She admitted that she'd gone into rages many times since the election, and that it had gotten so bad that she had to send the maid and cook home so they wouldn't see her in that state. She'd smashed some glasses and cut herself rather deeply. She told us that at one point she had gotten so angry she had nearly passed out, and Bill caught her just before she fell.

"She said that Bill had tried to be affectionate and get her mind off the loss. He held her hand, kissed her on the forehead, and tried to do everything he could to comfort her. But she told him to leave Chappaqua, because she was making him miserable. She insisted he go.

"Chelsea arrived without her kids. I was hoping she'd cheer up her mom. But instead, she started in on Trump, calling him 'that son of a bitch,' and Comey, and Hillary's 'idiotic' campaign staff, and even her dad, who she said never had his heart in the campaign.

"Late in the afternoon, Hillary switched from wine to gin and tonic. She got maudlin and talked about how her life was over. She said more than once, 'I won the goddam election!'"

■　■　■

On Inauguration Day, Melania Trump appeared in a powder-blue Ralph Lauren skirt suit, matching gloves, and stiletto shoes. Many famous designers—Tom Ford, Marc Jacobs, Zac Posen, Christian Siriano, and Sophie Theallet—hated Trump and refused to dress the new first lady. Moments after Melania was spotted by the TV cameras, the Internet exploded with a #BoycottRalphLauren hashtag. However, none of the disconcerted liberals seemed to mind in the least when Hillary Clinton showed up at the inauguration wearing a white Ralph Lauren pantsuit. Among the Trump haters, hypocrisy was never in short supply.

Hillary had dreaded the prospect of attending the inauguration.

"People close to her told me that she'd had doubts about being able to make it through without visibly losing control," wrote *New York* magazine's Rebecca Traister. "'Oh,' says Clinton, 'it was hard. It was really…difficult.' But 'at the time, we hoped that there would be a different agenda for governing than there had been for running.'

"A look of disgust crosses Clinton's face as she recalls [Trump's inaugural speech]," Traister continued. "'It was a really painful cry to his hard-core supporters that he wasn't changing,' she says. 'The "carnage" in our country? It was a very disturbing moment.[1] I caught Michelle Obama's eyes, like, *What is going on here*? I was sitting next to George and Laura Bush, and we have our political differences, but this was beyond any experience any of us had ever had.'

"I ask her about the report that Bush had said of the speech, 'That was some weird shit,' and her eyes light up. 'Put it in your article,' she says. 'They tried to walk back from it, but. . . .' Did she hear it herself? I ask. She raises her eyebrows and grins."

■ ■ ■

The resistance was out in full force during the inaugural ceremonies. Protesters swarmed onto the streets of Washington. Some of them threw bricks and bottles at the police, who responded with pepper spray and stun grenades. A limousine was set on fire. Windows were smashed. Municipal shelters were destroyed. The protesters, many of whom belonged to an anarchist group called Disruptj20, tried to block several of the entrances to the National Mall, where pro-Trump crowds were gathering to participate in the inauguration.

"At one gated entrance, protesters opposed to the completion of the Dakota Access oil pipeline linked arms through short pieces of PVC pipe known as lockboxes, a technique that helps keep them from being pulled apart by police," the *Wall Street Journal* reported. "After a warning, police dragged from the entrance a handful of protesters who hadn't brought lockboxes, and officers brought out electric hand-grinders to cut through the pipes to separate them."

In New York City, several hundred people gathered at Foley Square. They chanted "Black Lives Matter" and "education not deportation." In Chicago, mounted police blocked protesters from marching down swanky Lake Shore Drive. In Seattle, where a man was shot and crowds threw bricks at the police, the police department tweeted: "Officers working to remove one person with suspected gunshot wound to abdomen from crowd at UW campus demonstration."

"What I am hoping for is the beginning of some serious organizing on behalf of working and poor people," said Rose Brown, who handed out a newsletter for the Revolutionary Organization of Labor during a protest in Boston's historic Common.[2]

Anti-Trump celebrities used social media to attack the new president before he had a chance to take the oath of office. Among them was Chrissy Teigen, the model who is married to the singer and songwriter John Legend. Chrissy, who once sent a Snapchat selfie of her struggling to zip up a long-sleeved jumpsuit over her exposed breasts, mocked the pastor delivering the invocation at the inauguration by tweeting: "What a beautiful prayer. Makes me wanna grab my pussy."

"Had Hillary won, everyone would have expected disappointed Trump voters to show a modicum of respect for the election result as well as for the historic ceremony of the inauguration, during which former combatants momentarily unite to pay homage to the peaceful transition of power in our democracy," said the social critic Camille Paglia, who is a registered Democrat. "But that was not the reaction of a vast cadre of Democrats shocked by Trump's win.

"In an abject failure of leadership that may be one of the most disgraceful episodes in the history of the modern Democratic Party," Paglia continued, "Chuck Schumer, who had risen to become the Senate Democratic leader after the retirement of Harry Reid, asserted absolutely no moral authority as the party spun out of control in a nationwide orgy of rage and spite."

PART THREE

FIRST HUNDRED DAYS

21

TRUMP DERANGEMENT SYNDROME

The day after Donald Trump's inauguration, 200,000 demonstrators descended on Washington, DC to participate in what the organizers called the "Women's March." Four million others showed up at marches that were staged in major cities around the country. It was the biggest political protest in American history, and it unleashed the energies of the resistance movement like nothing had before.

Female demonstrators, who were in the majority, wore pink "pussy hats" and carried colorful handmade signs, which gave the march an improvised appearance. The mainstream media bought the claim that the event was a spontaneous uprising, "forming out of nowhere," in the words of lefty rabble-rouser Michael Moore.

But in fact many of the placards had been cranked out by volunteers, not by the marchers who carried them. Several of Hillary Clinton's veteran campaign advisers played a key role in organizing the march, the aim of which, besides trying to stir up feminist hate against the new Republican president, was to fight Trump's pledge to repeal and replace Obamacare, approve the Dakota Access and Keystone XL pipelines, and end federal subsidies to sanctuary cities. The activist women behind the march received assistance from labor union organizers and anti-Trump groups like Indivisible and Our Revolution, a spin-off from Bernie Sanders' presidential campaign.

The march had plenty of headliners, including Cher, Katy Perry, and Madonna, who announced, "Yes, I'm angry. Yes, I'm outraged. Yes, I have thought an awful lot of blowing up the White House."

Piers Morgan, who was taken aback by the extremism, foul language, and hypocrisy of the march, noted that "Actress Ashley Judd read out a young poet's attack on Trump, branding him the Devil and Hitler, mocking his hair and complexion, and cracking a crude…incest joke about him and his daughter Ivanka."

That was barely half of it; the "poem" also accused Trump of, among other things, "racism, fraud, conflict of interest, homophobia, sexual assault, transphobia, white supremacy, misogyny, ignorance, [and] white privilege."

Morgan concluded, "This was nasty women being nasty, whipped into a man-hating frenzy by some very nasty women on a stage."

It was ironic too that a march, dedicated in part to women's rights, should include among its organizers Linda Sansour, head of the Arab American Association of New York, who supports anti-feminist Sharia law and is a vocal critic of Israel, where women have far more rights than they do elsewhere in the Middle East.

But feminists, leftists, and supporters of Sharia law made common cause against Trump. When Trump announced that he was blocking all travel to the United States by citizens of seven Muslim-majority countries—seven nations identified by the Obama administration as among the most dangerous in the world—crowds began converging on airports across America. At Tom Bradley airport in Los Angeles, demonstrators chanted, "Let them in!" and "Love, not hate, makes America great."

"There was almost a carnival atmosphere as some protesters marched around the lower level of LAX beating drums, blowing whistles and chanting, 'No ban, no wall, sanctuary for all!'" reported James Queally, Javier Panzar, and Matt Hamilton in the *Los Angeles Times*.

Trump's executive order imposed a temporary freeze on all refugee admissions, a ban on travel from seven Muslim-majority countries, and the detention or deportation of hundreds of immigrants arriving at U.S. airports. His neophyte team in the West Wing, however, failed to subject the order to the normal agency review and legal vetting. As a result, legitimate green-card holders and loyal Iraqi civilians who had worked as interpreters for the U.S. military were banned from entering the United States. Immigration lawyers, funded by George Soros and working on behalf of the ACLU, spotted these errors and convinced a federal judge in New York to place a temporary stay on the order.[1]

"To be clear," Trump said in a written statement, "this is not a Muslim ban, as the media is falsely reporting. This is not about religion—this is about terror and keeping our country safe."

But the Democrats were in no mood to listen.

"The fury is…spurring liberal voters to demand uncompromising confrontation and resistance from their elected officials to a president they believe poses an existential threat to the country," Jonathan Martin of the *New York Times* wrote. "The Democrats' increasingly assertive base wants the party's leaders to eschew any cooperation with Mr. Trump: They are already expressing rage at some senators for confirming the president's cabinet appointees, and for their willingness to allow a vote on his pick for a vacant Supreme Court seat.

"The rush of Democratic governors and senators, both moderates and progressives, to airports this weekend also showed that they recognized that the outpouring of protesters for the women's marches on inauguration weekend was only the start of a new movement," Martin continued. "The demands for purity from Democratic leaders are likely to grow only more unequivocal, and standing in solidarity with sign-waving protesters may prove insufficient…. The scale and ferocity of the anger coming out of the Democratic base has astounded even some party veterans."

The atmosphere was ripe for hyperbole, and Vice President Joe Biden, a past master at taking someone else's ideas and passing them off as his own, spoke to the frenzied Democratic base.

"I remind people," said Biden, "'68 was really a bad year [but] America didn't break. It's as bad now, but I'm hopeful."

"It was telling that Biden had to sift through nearly a half century of history to find a precedent for the current malaise among liberals and progressives," wrote *The New Yorker's* Jelani Cobb in an article titled "The Return of Civil Disobedience."

In recent years, the once-witty and urbane *New Yorker* had taken a tedious turn to the left. The magazine's editor, David Remnick, conducted a holy war against Donald Trump from his desk at 1 World Trade Center, abandoning his conservative and middle-of-the-road readers and preaching exclusively to the Bernie Sanders-Elizabeth Warren-Kamala Harris wing of the Democratic Party.

"The election of Donald Trump," Remnick hyperventilated, "is nothing less than a tragedy for the American republic, a tragedy for the Constitution, and a triumph for the forces, at home and abroad, of nativism, authoritarianism, misogyny, and racism. Trump's shocking victory, his ascension to the Presidency, is a sickening event in the history of the United States and liberal democracy."

Words have consequences and journalists like Remnick helped unleash a political witch-hunt the likes of which hadn't been seen in America since the days of Joseph McCarthy. The incendiary words inflamed those with unhinged minds and led to outbreaks of violence and threats against the life of the president.

"By indulging their and their audience's rage, [the media] spread the rage," wrote the *Wall Street Journal's* Peggy Noonan. "They celebrate themselves as brave for this. They stood up to the man, they spoke truth to power. But what courage, really, does that take? Their audiences love it. Their base loves it, their demo loves it, their bosses love it. Their numbers go up. They get a better contract. This isn't brave."

New York magazine's Jonathan Chait was typical of the kind of voguish journalist Peggy Noonan had in mind. Ignoring the fact that FBI Director James Comey had assured Trump on three separate occasions that he was not under investigation in the Russian scandal, Chait wrote, "The scandal is spinning off in multiple directions, but at bottom it suggests a betrayal of American sovereignty by Trump that is unprecedented in the history of the republic."

There was no evidence that Donald Trump had, in any way, betrayed American sovereignty. In fact, his political platform was an unapologetic reassertion of American sovereignty, which is why it had drawn such ire from liberal internationalists and Republican Never-Trumpers who deemed it "nationalist," "nativist," and "isolationist." The only thing unprecedented in the history of the republic was Trump Derangement Syndrome.

22

PSYCHOBABBLE

I f you listened to the rageaholics in the anti-Trump movement, it wasn't they who were deranged; it was Donald Trump.

From day one of the Trump presidency, the media broadcast the resistance's rallying cry that Trump was mentally unfit to occupy the Oval Office. Leftwing psychiatrists, psychologists, and other mental health professionals jumped on the bandwagon in support of the Trump-Is-Nuts charge; more than 55,000 of them signed a petition claiming that Trump "manifests a serious mental illness."

Trump exhibited "textbook narcissistic personality disorder," Ben Michaelis, a clinical psychologist, told *Vanity Fair's* "Hive" contributor Henry Alford. Added George Simon, another psychologist interviewed by Alford: "He's so classic that I'm archiving video clips of him to use in workshops because there's no better example. Otherwise I would have had to hire actors and write vignettes. He's like a dream come true."

There were serious problems with this effort to put the new president on the couch. To begin with, it violated a code of ethics known as the Goldwater Rule, which was adopted by the American Psychiatric Association in 1973 and which condemned diagnosing public figures at a distance.[1]

More important, Allen Frances, a professor emeritus of psychiatry and behavioral sciences at Duke University, and the reigning expert on narcissistic personality disorder, wrote a stinging letter to the *New York Times* disputing his colleagues' diagnosis.

"Most amateur diagnosticians have mislabeled President Trump with the diagnosis of narcissistic personality disorder," Frances stated. "I wrote the criteria that define this disorder [in the *Diagnostic and Statistical Manual of Mental Disorders*], and Mr. Trump doesn't meet them. He may be a world-class narcissist, but this doesn't make him mentally ill, because he does not suffer from the distress and impairment to diagnose mental disorder."

What the anti-Trump psychiatrists and psychologists were describing was not mental illness, but behavior they disapproved of.

"In the first debate, [Trump] talked over people and was domineering," complained Charlotte Proznan, a psychotherapist. "He'll do anything to demean others, like tell Carly Fiorina he doesn't like her looks. 'You're fired!' would certainly come under lack of empathy. And he wants to deport immigrants, but [two of] his wives have been immigrants."

To which Duke University's Allen Frances replied: "Bad behavior is rarely a sign of mental illness, and the mentally ill behave badly only rarely."

Ironically, the criticism leveled at Trump could just as easily have been directed at Barack Obama. For example, Dr. Lynne Meyer, a Beverly Hills psychologist, noted that Trump, like Obama, was "quickly bored by and dismissive of anything that does not have to do with himself."

"Excuse me while I duck out and laugh," wrote the *Washington Times*' Cheryl K. Chumley. "But did we not just come off eight years of King Obama, Man of the Hubris? The guy couldn't open his mouth without spewing arrogance. Heck, in most cases, he didn't even have to open his mouth—he just had to be. Remember the selfie heard round the world, when Obama, in the middle of Nelson Mandela's memorial service, slid tight toward the blond Danish prime minister, Helle Thorning-Schmidt, to take a quick pic? Or, the equally 'I'm More Important Than You' moment when he cavalierly handed off an umbrella to a nearby Marine to hold—dress standards of the Corps be danged—and casually slipped his rain-droopy self under its shield and continued his speech? Actions speak louder than words, as they say."

Finally, what seemed to trouble the mental health professionals even more than Trump himself was the psychological state of his supporters.

Said Harvard's Howard Gardner: "They are unable or unwilling to make a connection between the challenges faced by any president and the knowledge and behavior of Donald Trump."

In short, the psychiatrists and psychologists didn't like Donald Trump and his supporters because, in the elitist neologism of Hillary Clinton, they were "The Deplorables."

23

ALL OUT WAR

I n February, the beaten and demoralized leaders of the Democratic Party gathered to choose a new party chairman. The race was between two hotheaded leftists: Representative Keith Ellison, who had ties to the anti-white, anti-Semitic Nation of Islam, and former Labor Secretary Tom Perez, whom one of the party's biggest donors, Haim Saban, described as "an anti-Semite." Jonathan Martin and Alexander Burns noted in the *New York Times* that it probably didn't matter which man won (Perez ultimately got the nod), because "the blueprint [for rebuilding the party] has already been chosen [by] an incensed army of liberals demanding no less than total war against President Trump."

The war against Trump was waged on three fronts:

- The Deep State
- The Congress
- The Streets

The Deep State

There was a Niagara of anti-Trump leaks from the moment Donald Trump won the election. Many of these leaks originated in the seventeen agencies that comprised the intelligence community; others came from Congress, the federal departments and agencies, and the White House.

The leaks came so fast and furious that it was hard to keep up with them. They included:

- General Michael Flynn's phone conversations with Russian Ambassador Sergey Kislyak regarding U.S. sanctions against Moscow
- President Trump's phone conversations with the presidents of Mexico and Australia
- Attorney General Jeff Sessions meeting with Kislyak during the 2016 campaign
- Trump's alleged disclosure of highly classified intelligence to Kislyak and Russian Foreign Minister Sergey Lavrov
- Jared Kushner's phone conversation with Kislyak regarding setting up a back channel between Washington and the Kremlin
- Secretary of Commerce Wilbur Ross's conversation with Trump about food safety
- Trump's proposed executive order cutting back the budget of the Environmental Protection Agency by $2 billion
- The FBI's investigation of Paul Manafort's alleged contacts with Russian intelligence agents
- The scurrilous—and widely discredited—British dossier of Trump's illicit behavior in Moscow
- The expansion of Special Counsel Robert Mueller's investigation of the Trump campaign's alleged ties to Russia to include Trump's previous business dealings and possible obstruction of justice

Such leaks—all of them illegal and based on anonymous sources—found their way with alarming regularity onto the front pages of the *Washington Post*, the *New York Times*, and the *Los Angeles Times*, and on the nightly newscasts of the major broadcast and cable networks.[1] This cascade of negative stories led President Trump to charge that the leaks were part of a Deep State conspiracy to destroy his presidency.

The mainstream media cast doubt on the existence of the Deep State—rogue elements within the permanent federal bureaucracy, many of them holdovers from the Obama administration, who operated on a clandestine basis against the White House. Few people, however, doubted that many of the leaks bore the unmistakable hallmark of the U.S. intelligence community. Trump compared these defamatory leaks to the big lie tactics of the Nazis.[2]

In January, Chuck Schumer virtually acknowledged the existence of the Deep State when he told MSNBC's Rachel Maddow that Trump would regret his attack on the intelligence community.

"Let me tell you, you take on the intelligence community, they have six ways from Sunday at getting back at you," said Schumer. "So even for a practical, supposedly hard-nosed businessman, [Trump's] being really dumb to do this."

Newt Gingrich was a believer in the Deep State.

"Of course the Deep State exists," he said. "There's a permanent state of massive bureaucracies that do whatever they want and set up deliberate leaks to attack the president. This is what the Deep State does. They create a lie, spread a lie, fail to check the lie, and then deny they were behind the lie."

Later, Gingrich tweeted: "[Special counsel Robert] Mueller is now clearly the tip of the Deep State spear aimed at destroying or at a minimum undermining and crippling the Trump presidency."

Disruptions caused by members of the Deep State were conspicuous in the Interior Department, the Environmental Protection Agency, and the Department of Justice. Attorney General Jeff Sessions read his top staff the riot act when he learned that disloyal employees with access to secure government files were deleting computer files and destroying evidence in an effort to impede the Justice Department's investigations of sanctuary cities and violent left-wing groups.

The most powerful evidence concerning the existence of the Deep State came from the Federal Bureau of Investigation. After conducting 2,000 interviews, the FBI's field offices in Los Angeles, San Francisco, Detroit, and New York compiled a 1,400-word report for Director James Comey on the people and groups influencing the resistance movement. The field report is being published for the first time in this book.[3]

"The Bureau has gotten actionable intelligence that there is, within the federal government, a growing and organized movement to block or interfere with administration policy decisions," the memo states.

"There have been regular organized meetings of large numbers of government workers at a church in the Columbia Heights area of the District [of Columbia] where plans have been discussed to actively sabotage government programs they disagree with," the memo continues. "These would include immigration enforcement, crackdowns on welfare fraud and any weakening of environmental rules. Plus, there is concern that some dissenting government workers might be dislodged from their positions by the Trump Administration.

"There is evidence that, while there is a great deal of agitation within the government, there are non-government individuals associated with unions and immigration and environmental groups who are behind these meetings.

"Legal groups have been teaching some of these government employees what they can get away with doing in terms of delaying enforcement and what they cannot in terms of refusing to obey orders, which would constitute going on strike and get them dismissed under civil service rules.

"One management level government employee said, 'Bureaucrats are going to delay, drag their feet and throw roadblocks in the way of unconscionable actions by the Trump White House. It is going to become impossible to get these actions done.'"

The Congress

"With few tools at their disposal, [congressional] Democrats have resorted to guerrilla tactics to delay Trump's agenda and inflict damage on him and his administration," Andy Kroll wrote in *Rolling Stone*. "[The Democrats] held shadow confirmation hearings that featured witnesses Republicans refused to allow to testify in the formal confirmation process. At one such hearing, homeowners testified about the shoddy foreclosure practices of OneWest, the troubled bank that Steven Mnuchin [Trump's then-nominee for treasury secretary] and others investors bought and later flipped for $3.4 billion.

"The Mnuchin attacks," Kroll continued, "highlighted an inside-outside strategy that has been essential to Democrats' early anti-Trump efforts.... Emboldened by the airport protests, Democrats agreed to drag out the confirmation process by boycotting committee votes and using procedural motions to delay final votes on Trump's nominees."

The first shot in the confirmation battle was fired by Kirsten Gillibrand, New York's foul-mouthed, junior Democratic senator, who had arrived in the upper chamber in 2009 as a moderate and, sensing the way the wind was blowing, mutated into a full-bore anti-Trump liberal.

"If we are not helping people, we should go the fuck home," Gillibrand told an audience at New York University. "Has [Trump] kept any of these promises? No. Fucking no."

Gillibrand picked as her target James "Mad Dog" Mattis—a retired Marine Corps four-star general, highly regarded for his intellect and devotion to duty by members of Congress on both sides of the aisle—whom Trump had nominated for secretary of defense. She forced a roll-call vote, which gave her the opportunity to be the sole senator opposing his appointment—an unambiguous display of ambition that was calculated to advance her prospects as a presidential candidate in 2020.

Just as Mattis was easily confirmed, so were retired Marine Corps General John Kelly as secretary of Homeland Security; former congressman Mike Pompeo as director of the Central Intelligence Agency; and former governor Nikki Haley as ambassador to the United Nations.

But the Democrats were picking their shots and had chosen Elizabeth DeVos and Jeff Sessions as their main targets. DeVos, a respected school-choice activist and Trump's nominee for secretary of education, was married to the heir of the Amway fortune and was the sister of Erik Prince, the founder of the private security company Blackwater—a liberal bogeyman if ever there was one. Senator Jeff Sessions, Trump's choice for attorney general, had been blocked before by the Democrats—in 1986, when President Ronald Reagan had nominated him for a federal judgeship—and the Democrats in the Senate, his former colleagues, were eager to torpedo him again.

"The Democrats called for an all-night marathon debate of DeVos's nomination leading up the vote on Feb.7," Charles Homans reported in the *New York Times Magazine.* "It wasn't a filibuster—[former Democratic majority leader Harry] Reid had done away with those for cabinet nominees in 2013—but a kind of sit-in: an effort to draw attention to the vote in hopes of further overloading the Senate office buildings' phone lines and nudging off the fence one of several Republican senators who had been identified, perhaps wishfully, as potentially persuadable.... [As Ezra Levin noted] 'In the two weeks between Pompeo and DeVos, there were massive protests. And zero Democrats voted for DeVos... .'

"The next day," Homans continued, "at a confirmation hearing for Jeff Sessions, Elizabeth Warren read from a letter that Coretta Scott King wrote in 1986 opposing his judicial appointment, prompting [Majority Leader Mitch] McConnell to censure her with an obscure procedural rule. McConnell's justification—"She was warned; she was given an explanation; nevertheless, she persisted"—quickly evolved into a rallying cry [for the anti-Trump forces], prompting nearly twice as many Google searches for Warren's name as her election to the Senate did in 2012. In the next 24 hours, members of the grass-roots organization MoveOn raised $300,000 for her 2018 re-election campaign, and Sessions [and DeVos were] confirmed."[4]

The Democrats were counting on their strategy to pay off in the 2018 midterm elections. They needed to gain twenty-four seats in order to capture control of the House of Representatives. They made no secret of their intentions if they were successful in taking over the House: they would immediately bring articles of impeachment against President Trump.

But the delay-delay-delay "inside game" in Congress was only one part of the Democrats' "resistance" to the president of the United States. Goaded on by Elizabeth Warren, the party's leftist base wanted action.

"Let's start with a simple fact," Warren told the annual retreat of the Congressional Progressive Caucus. "It's time for Democrats to grow a backbone and get out there and fight!" Plenty of Democrat "progressives" took her at her word.

The Streets

"We will fight like dogs in the street," vowed Michael Brune, the executive director of the Sierra Club. He wasn't kidding.

Almost from its commencement, violent demonstrators—some, we now know, paid for by Democratic operatives—harassed the Trump campaign and its supporters; and the violence never stopped, not after the election, and not after the inauguration. If anything, the resistance movement, with the apparent blessing of the Democratic Party, increasingly resorted to violence. In April, members of an organization called Antifa, which stood for "anti-fascist action," attacked a pro-Trump demonstration at the University of California, Berkeley. Journalist Lauren Southern shot a video showing Antifa street fighters throwing bricks and M-80 explosives into the crowd.

"Not getting disarmed is a big part of the problem, yes, but we need more than flags and bats," one of the thugs wrote on the group's subreddit community page. "We need to take notes from the John Brown Gun Club and get firearms and training."

In Pennsylvania, "a woman associated with Antifa attacked a police horse, using a flagpole with nails extending out from it," said Judson Phillips, the founder of Tea Party Nation. "At the same incident in

Pennsylvania, other Antifa terrorists had sharpened bamboo poles and baseball bats. The weapons have ranged from glitter-filled gel to urine bombs, to chains, bicycle locks, and baseball bats.

"The same Antifa group has made college campuses virtually a 'no-go' zone for conservatives," Phillips continued. "Noted conservatives such as Ann Coulter, Milo Yiannopoulos and Ben Shapiro cannot go onto many college campuses to speak without having their events disrupted to the point the event cannot go on."[5]

After Trump's victory, gun shop owners braced for a fall-off in sales because, they reasoned, conservatives would no longer feel the need to arm themselves against the fallout from a Hillary Clinton presidency. However, on Black Friday, the day after Thanksgiving Day, 185,713 people applied for firearm background checks—a twenty-year record for a single day—and many them were liberals who had previously been in favor of scrapping the Second Amendment.

"Some of those gun buyers are what the industry calls 'non-traditional,'" wrote McClatchy's Teresa Welsh. "Namely, minorities, gay people, and self-described liberals."

Welsh interviewed a spokeswoman for the Liberal Gun Club, which described itself as a shooting group that "honors diversity," teaches "queers to shoot," and trained members of groups such as Black Guns Matter and Pink Pistols.

Violent threats were made against several Republican House members, including Tom Garrett, who had to cancel his scheduled town halls after he received a message warning, "This is how we're going to kill your wife." An anti-Trump activist tried to drive Tennessee Congressman David Kustoff's car off the road. And in the most notorious incident, James Hodgkinson, a volunteer with Bernie Sanders' failed presidential campaign, tracked congressional Republicans to a baseball practice for the annual congressional baseball game, and shot and seriously wounded Louisiana Representative Steve Scalise, as well as wounding two police officers, a congressional staffer, and a lobbyist.[6]

The FBI had its eyes on members of radical groups, some of whom received combat training "nearly on a par with ISIS training, minus the suicide bombs," according to the confidential FBI report on the resistance.[7] The report also compared the training and preparation to that of the Black Panthers when they threatened domestic terrorism in the 1970s.

"Of [great] concern is the Berkeley-based militant group [called] It's Going Down, which has cells that communicate through the Internet from colleges in all 50 states, as well as Canada and Mexico," the FBI report said. "This organization has accepted responsibility for the violence and destruction in Berkeley, despite comments by Professor Robert Reich and UC Berkeley Police Chief Margo Bennett that the incidents were performed by 'outside agitators.' One of the arrestees in the incidents was identified as a student of Professor Reich."

"This organization is under active investigation by the Bureau owing to their interstate funding nature and their inclination to physically attack banks and savings and loans with fire bombs, rocks and iron rods," the report continued. "They raise funds through PayPal and Bitcoin.

"It's Going Down has been active since late 2015, publishes a magazine and videos encouraging violent demonstrations against banks and other institutions. They refer to their organization as anarchist, and say they collect funds to finance 'uprisings and rebellions.' It bills itself as an 'anarchist' group and claims ties to other violent anarchist groups abroad, including [in] Peru. [A stamp on the report says "Action Required."]

"It is recommended that all intelligence the bureau gathers on this organization be shared with the Secret Service.

"There are numerous off-shoot organizations of It's Going Down, including Final Straw, which advocates for the release of federal prisoners who have been convicted of sabotage, arson, bank robbery, and bombing. At the top of the list, which has been widely disseminated on various web sites, are Joan Laman, who was convicted of armed robbery and bank robbery in the 1980s, and is serving a fifty-year term in federal prison. Another on recent posts is Marius Mason, who is serving time for sabotage and arson.

"There is no evidence that this group has done more than petition for the release of these federal prisoners. There is no evidence they have tried to organize a prison escape. But they are obviously encouraging violent activism by heralding their crimes.

"Funding for this group includes small donations sent through bitcoin and PayPal. They use their funding to record podcasts and regular hour-long radio broadcasts on community radio stations ranging from Asheville, NC, to Fairbanks, AK.

"Some funding also comes from George Soros, who they refer to in their fund raising broadcasts and literature as 'Daddy Warbucks.'

"The organization and its subgroups advocate workouts for its members, and training to engage in 'street fighting.' It is clear that their motives include preparing members, both male and female, to engage in hand-to-hand combat with police and guards of banks and other financial institutions.

"Several members of the group, arrested in the fire-bombing and sabotage in Berkeley, described to local police and later FBI agents the nature of the training they received, which included the making of Molotov cocktails and the use of tire irons among other weaponized tools to do the most destruction possible, and [the] use [of] weapons against law enforcement personnel who get in their way.

"The training, which takes place often in public gyms that are sympathetic to the cause, particularly in the San Francisco Bay Area, is unprecedented in recent years....

"The organization complains about the 'liberal fetishization of nonviolence' in its writing online, and claims 'they are more interested in doing what is right, not what is legal.'"

The report continues, "There is intelligence the group and/or off-shoots are planning a training camp in rural Massachusetts over the summer.

"There have always been militant groups, particularly associated with UC Berkeley, but the agitprop against the current administration is unusually virulent, and potentially dangerous.

"There have been intercepts recently that the organization is in contact with Muslim militants both in Detroit and overseas. There was a suggestion that they wish to liaise with some radical elements with the hope of learning more aggressive and violent tactics. This group has made common cause against Islamic Americans who have come out against any imposition of Sharia Law in the U.S., which intel suggests is a condition to get cooperation from extremists.

"This is a concern that is actionable and must be closely monitored."

24

THE IMPEACHMENT BANDWAGON

You didn't have to read beyond the headlines to understand that the villains were obsessed with impeaching President Trump.

- "The campaign to impeach President Trump has begun"— the *Washington Post*, January 20, 2017
- "Will Donald Trump Make It a Year in Office?"— *Vanity Fair, The Hive*, January 25, 2017
- "Legal Scholars: Why Congress Should Impeach Donald Trump"—*Time* magazine, February 6, 2017
- "Trump Impeached? You Can Bet on It"—*Politico*, February 12, 2017
- "House Democrat From California Seeks Support to Impeach Trump"—the *New York Times*, June 12, 2017
- "Democrats Hatch Plans A, B, and C to Impeach Trump"—*The Daily Signal*, July 10, 2017

At the very moment that Chief Justice John Roberts was administering the Oath of Office to Trump, impeachtrumpnow.org went live on the Internet. Within forty-eight hours, more than 100,000 people had signed the website's petition. By the fall of 2017, the site had collected several million signatures.

The site was run by two "resistance" groups—Free Speech for People and RootsAction—both of which were supported and funded by George Soros' Open Society Foundations, David Brock's Citizens for Responsibility and Ethics in Washington (CREW), and Priorities USA Action, the largest Democratic Party super PAC. Two of the leaders of Free Speech for People—Lance Lindblom, a director, and Jeff Clements, a co-founder of the group and its general counsel—were old Soros hands. Lindblom was the former executive vice president of Soros' Open Society Institute/Open Society Fund, and Clements attended Soros' board meetings.

A key figure in the impeachment movement was Norman Solomon, the co-founder of RootsAction.[1] The mainstream media barely mentioned Solomon in its coverage of the "resistance," which wasn't surprising given the fact that reporters failed to investigate the movement, its leaders, its ideology, and its funding.

The sixty-six-year-old Solomon was a high school drop-out who had been on and off the FBI's watch list since he was fourteen. He was an avowed socialist, who wrote a book criticizing the comic strip *Dilbert* as a capitalist tool. He visited Moscow eight times before the fall of the Soviet Union.

Solomon's group, RootsAction, epitomized what might be called the "demented" wing of the "resistance."[2] Among its screwiest ideas, it presented a petition to the Nobel Institute recommending that the Nobel Peace Prize be awarded to none other than Bradley Manning—also known as Chelsea Manning—the former U.S. Army intelligence analyst, who was sentenced to thirty-five years in prison for stealing hundreds of thousands of military secrets and giving them to WikiLeaks.[3]

■ ▓ ▓

The villains' drive for impeachment was like a marathon run on a treadmill; it broke a sweat but got nowhere. The rationale the villains offered for impeachment was confusing, changeable, inconsistent, and bordered on the ridiculous. For instance, in his book *The Case for Impeachment*, Allan Lichtman, an American University professor, maintained that Trump could be impeached for crimes against humanity because he refused to abide by the Paris Climate Accord—an agreement that was legally unenforceable and posed a threat to the U.S. economy.

Stripped of its tiresome verbiage, the villains' case for impeachment boiled down to three propositions:

1. The George Soros crowd argued that Trump obstructed justice by firing the director of the FBI.
2. Democrats in Congress charged that Trump violated the Constitution by receiving profits, or "emoluments," from foreign officials who were guests at his hotel in Washington, DC.
3. The media promoted the view that Trump should be thrown out of office because he had colluded with the Russians during the presidential election campaign.

Let's examine these propositions one by one:

Proposition No. 1—the obstruction of justice argument—was easily dispensed with.

"The president has the authority to direct the head of the FBI to stop investigating anyone," said Alan Dershowitz, a former Harvard Law professor and a lifelong Democrat. "I think this puts an end to any claim that President Trump obstructed justice. You can't obstruct justice by simply exercising your power under the Constitution."

"Under the Constitution, the president has the absolute power to fire principal officers, such as Director Comey," said Josh Blackman, a constitutional law professor at the South Texas College of Law in Houston. "Indeed, the termination was accompanied by a fairly elaborate set of reasons by the deputy attorney general."

Proposition No. 2—the so-called "emolument" argument—was refuted by a careful reading of Article I, Section 9, Clause 8 of the Constitution. This clause states that "no Person holding any Office of Profit or Trust under them, shall, without the Consent of the Congress, accept of any present, Emolument, Office, or Title, of any kind whatever, from any King, Prince, or foreign state."

Put in modern English, the emoluments clause sought to shield the United States from corrupting foreign influences.

In Congress, Brad Sherman of California and Al Green of Texas invoked the emoluments clause when they introduced articles of impeachment against the president. Their case rested on the dubious argument that, because of Trump's sprawling business empire, he was in direct violation of Article I, Section 9, Clause 8 of the Constitution.

"The most immediate concern," wrote *USA Today's* Heidi M. Przbyla, "has been foreign diplomats booking hotels and conference rooms at Trump hotel properties in order to curry favor with him."

The New Yorker magazine devoted 9,900 words to an article titled "How Trump Could Get Fired." It cited a federal lawsuit, filed by David Brock's Citizens for Responsibility and Ethics in Washington, that accused Trump of violating the emoluments clause. "The lawsuit," wrote Evan Osnos, the author of the article, "cites the Trump International Hotel, half a mile from the White House, which foreign dignitaries have admitted frequenting as a way to curry favor with the President."

Trump, however, disposed of this argument by promising to donate the proceeds from foreign hotel guests to the U.S. Treasury. And, in any case, Andy Grewal, the Joseph F. Rosenfield Fellow in Law at the University of Iowa, marshaled a powerful legal case that "emoluments" was limited to salary and other financial benefits, and didn't cover private business interests.

"Grewal's view," reported the *National Review's* Dan McLaughlin, "receives significant additional support from a new originalist analysis by retired University of Montana law professor Robert Natelson, author of *The Original Constitution: What It Actually Said and Meant....* Among other things, Professor Natelson [argues that the pro-impeachment rationale] would have eliminated Virginia tobacco planters like Thomas Jefferson or James Madison from ever being considered for the presidency, given the nature of state involvement in the tobacco business at the time."[4]

Proposition No. 3—the collusion argument—gained traction when Trump met in the Oval Office with Russia's ambassador Sergey Kislyak and his boss, Foreign Minister Sergey Lavrov. Someone with first-hand knowledge of that meeting—presumably a White House official—told the *Washington Post* that the president had shared classified information about ISIS with the Russians.

"The cries to impeach Trump grew louder, even after he tweeted... that he had 'the absolute right' to 'share with Russia,'" reported *Newsweek*. "Former CIA Director Leon Panetta chastised the president in blunt terms on CNN, arguing that 'he cannot just say whatever the hell he wants and expect it doesn't carry consequences.'"

"In the United States, no one is above the law," wrote MoveOn.org's Anna Galland. "The testimony that former FBI Director James Comey is expected to deliver today makes clear that Congress must begin impeachment proceedings immediately. Today's testimony puts us in fundamentally new territory. This is no longer about our opposition to Trump's policies and rhetoric."

The collusion argument picked up steam after it was revealed that Donald Trump Jr. met in Trump Tower during the presidential campaign with Natalia Veselnitskaya, a Russian lawyer connected to the Kremlin, and a sketchy Russian-American lobbyist. The Russians arranged the meeting by promising to reveal dirt on Hillary Clinton, but within the first few minutes it became clear that they didn't have any dirt. Their real motive was to lobby the Trump campaign to push for repeal of United States sanctions imposed on certain Russian officials by the 2012 Magnitsky Act.

Trump Jr. later admitted that he shouldn't have taken the meeting, and he released the email chain that led up to the meeting. He acknowledged that everyone quickly realized that the meeting was a waste of time, that no information about Hillary Clinton cooperating with the Russians was divulged, that the entire meeting lasted only twenty minutes, and that there was no further contact between him and the Russians.

Nonetheless, Democrats seized on the meeting as prima facie evidence that members of the Trump campaign were in cahoots with the Kremlin. And they filled the TV airwaves with verbal overkill.

"This is moving into perjury, false statements and even potentially treason," said Senator Tim Kaine, Hillary's running mate.

Nonsense! said Jonathan Turley, a professor at George Washington University Law School and a highly respected legal analyst.

"Washington began its week again with its collective Rorschach test: another Russian-related meeting that was immediately declared to be the 'smoking gun' of criminal collusion or even 'treason,'" Turley wrote in *The Hill*. "Article III defines treason as 'levying war against [the United States], or in adhering to their Enemies, giving them Aid and Comfort.' Trump Jr. went to a meeting on the belief that a lawyer had evidence of criminal collusion by Clinton with a foreign power. That is a rather curious basis for a charge of treason and would make traitors of countless campaign operatives."

There was, in sum, no smoking gun proving that the Trump campaign had colluded with the Kremlin. But there was a developing narrative that perhaps the Clinton campaign had done just that.

"Here's a thought," wrote Kimberley A. Strassel of the *Wall Street Journal*. "What if it was the Democratic National Committee or Hillary Clinton's campaign [that hired Fusion GPS]? What if that money flowed from a political entity on the left, to a private law firm, to Fusion, to a British spook, and then to Russian sources?"

Indeed, it looked increasingly as if the Democrats' Russia obsession could backfire; the only collusion for which there was any real evidence was of the Democrats reading the Fusion GPS dossier—based on Russian intelligence disinformation—into the *Congressional Record*. Perhaps it was time, then, for the Justice Department to appoint another special counsel to look into *Hillary Clinton's* ties to the Russians.

That was certainly President Trump's view. As he pointed out, it was not he who had extensive financial dealings with the Russians. It was the Clinton Foundation that received $145 million from uranium investors with ties to Russia. And it was Bill Clinton who received $500,000 for a speech in Russia after Secretary of State Clinton approved the sale of 20 percent of America's uranium production to a Russian-controlled company. Moreover, Hillary's campaign chairman, John Podesta, sat on the board of an energy company that had millions of dollars in investments from a Russian government fund.

■ ■ ■

The most intemperate impeachment advocate was California Democrat Maxine Waters, who led a "Tax March" in Washington, and declared: "I don't respect this president. I don't trust this president. He's not working in the best interests of the American people. I will fight every day until he is impeached."

Like many others, Waters exploited talk of impeachment as a way to promote herself and raise her profile in the media.

"Representative Maxine Waters has been reborn at the age of 78, emerging as a folk hero to the anti-Trump resistance for her repeated torching of the president," Lachlan Markay and Asawin Suebsaeng wrote in the *Daily Beast*. "From the glowing coverage and partisan praise, you'd barely detect that just a few years ago the veteran California congresswoman was dubbed one of the nation's 'most corrupt' elected officials by the Citizens for Responsibility and Ethics in Washington for her role in pushing a bailout for a bank tied to her family.

"Waters was eventually cleared by investigators," the writers continued, "though her grandson who served as her chief of staff was not. And now, Democrats seem to be embracing—and some liberal ethics advocates willfully ignoring—her sudden emergence as one of the nation's leading critics of ethical lapses in President Donald Trump's administration."

Waters' anti-Trump rants were so ungrammatical and irrational that they were often impossible to comprehend. For instance, she delivered the following gibberish:

"How can a president, who is acting in the manner that he is acting, whether he is talking about the travel ban, the way he is talking Muslims, or whether he's talking about his relationship to Putin and the Kremlin—knowing that they have hacked our DCCC and DNC and knowing that he is responsible for supplying the bombs that killed innocent children and families in Aleppo—the fact that he is wrapping his arms around Putin while Putin is continuing to advance into Korea... ."

"The liberal tirades about impeaching Trump remind me of dolphin sounds," said a political operative, whose experience in Washington went back decades. "They appeal to people who love dolphins because it makes them feel good about themselves, but they are unintelligible to normal humans."

■ ■ ■

It wasn't only Democrats who were caught up in the impeachment madness. Senator John McCain couldn't resist weighing in.

"I think it's reaching the point where it's of Watergate size and scale, and a couple of other scandals we've seen," said McCain, one of the most prominent Never-Trump Republicans.

McCain's comment drew immediate criticism from a number of sources, including former Assistant FBI Director James Kallstrom and radio talk show host Laura Ingraham.

"He's doing Chuck Schumer's work for him," Ingraham said. "You don't need the DNC when you've got John McCain."

McCain had never forgiven Trump for questioning his heroism. As chairman of the Senate Armed Services Committee, McCain called for a bipartisan select committee to investigate the Trump campaign's ties to the Kremlin.

Former Nixon adviser David Gergen, another member of the Never-Trump Republican brigade, naturally agreed with McCain.

"I must say, I was in the Nixon administration as you know and I thought after watching the Clinton impeachment, I thought I'd never see another one," said Gergen. "But I think we're in impeachment territory for the first time [with Trump]."

A nonprofit organization called Stand Up Republic launched a campaign, funded by a six-figure television buy, to convince Republicans to get behind the select committee effort to investigate Trump. Their suggestion for chairman: Senator Lindsey Graham, another Never-Trump Republican.

■ ■ ■

With Republicans in firm control of the House of Representatives, Trump seemed safe from impeachment. Article I of the Constitution gives sole power of impeachment to the House and the power to try impeachment to the Senate. Conviction in the Senate requires a two-thirds majority vote, which seemed out of the question in the current circumstances, because Republicans controlled the Senate with fifty-two seats to the Democrats' forty-eight.

"As long as Trump has a strong base behind him," said a Republican congressional aide, "I don't think it's smart for most [Republican] members to go out of their way to try and undermine him."

"Because the Republican leadership in the House of Representatives will almost certainly not initiate the ouster of a Republican president, the first step in any realistic path to impeachment is for the Democrats to gain control of the House," *The New Yorker*'s Evan Osnos wrote. "The next opportunity is the 2018 midterm elections."

That opportunity could easily be squandered by the Democrats, who had become a Johnny-one-note political party; the only thing they stood for was standing against Donald Trump. And that, most political observers agreed, was not a formula for success at the ballot box.

However, Democrats could not be counted out in 2018; historically, the party that controlled the White House lost congressional seats in midterm elections. And therein lay Trump's vulnerability, for should the Democrats gain control of the House in 2018 (they needed to pick up twenty-four seats) they would almost certainly start impeachment proceedings immediately.

"If the gavel changes hands, it's a different world," said Thomas M. Davis III, a former seven-term Republican congressman from Virginia and currently a professor at George Mason University. "No. 1, all of

[Trump's] public records—[the Democrats] will go through those with a fine-tooth comb: income taxes, business dealings. At that point, it's not just talk—they subpoena it. It gets ugly real fast."

25

"THIS IS WHAT A COUP LOOKS LIKE"

With impeachment the longest of long shots, the villains needed to come up with another strategy. They zeroed in on Section 4 of the Twenty-Fifth Amendment to the Constitution, under which the Cabinet can vote to remove the president and replace him with the vice president if the president is "unable to discharge the powers and duties of his office."

But how to prove that Trump was "disabled"?

A favorite mantra among members of the "resistance" was that Trump was too mentally ill to perform the duties of president. The villains pointed to a petition signed by fifty thousand psychiatrists, psychologists, and social workers that called Trump's mental health into question and urged his removal from office.

To the objection that none of these mental health professionals had examined Trump and therefore were in no position to diagnose him,

Lance Dodes, a retired Harvard professor of psychiatry, spoke for the dump-Trump-at-all-costs crowd.

"Trump is going to face challenges from people who are not going to bend to his will," said Dodes. "If you have a president who takes it as a personal attack on him, which he does, and flies into a paranoid rage, that's how you start a war."

The award-winning TV journalist Jeff Greenfield dismissed the idea that Trump could be removed on the basis of mental illness as a "liberal fantasy."

Laurence Tribe, a leftwing professor of law at Harvard, disagreed.

"I believe that invoking Section 4 of the Twenty-Fifth Amendment is no fantasy but an entirely plausible tool—not immediately, but well before 2020," Tribe said.

"If a coup d'état came to America it would look like this: unelected bureaucrats voting to remove a president because of his hostility to their jobs and his childlike temperament in expressing and executing his agenda," wrote Dominic Lynch in *Commentary* magazine. "President Trump is many things: an oaf, a buffoon and an incompetent politician. But he is also an existential threat to the culture of Washington, D.C., and its elites. His call to 'drain the swamp,' whether he means it or not, has obviously riled his base and whatever base elites still have to ground themselves on. This goes a long way to explaining the rage that encompasses the coastal media and its enablers.

"Nonetheless, the white-hot rage that has been brewing among the president's detractors since November 8, 2016, seems to be reaching a point not seen since the release of the 'Access Hollywood' tape a month before the election," Lynch continued. "Now, instead of calls for Trump to drop out of the race, there are calls for him to be removed by the Cabinet or impeached.

"But these are unstable times and these are dangerous ideas. In an election that—fairly or not—cast doubt on the presidency's legitimacy, in a political environment that careens between incompetence by Republicans and obstruction by Democrats, in a country whose social fabric is fraying, the calls to remove the president are reckless at best and damning at worst."

Charles Krauthammer agreed, saying the Democrats' invocation of Section 4 of the Twenty-Fifth Amendment "perverts the very intent of the amendment. It was meant for a stroke, not stupidity; for Alzheimer's, not narcissism. Otherwise, what it authorizes is a coup—willful overthrow by the leader's own closest associates.... Moreover, this would be seen by millions as an establishment usurpation to get rid of a disruptive outsider. It would be the most destabilizing event in American political history—the gratuitous overthrow of an essential constant in American politics, namely the fixedness of the presidential term (save for high crimes and misdemeanors)."

26

WHERE IN THE WORLD IS OBAMA?

"**B**arack wants to go back to his youth," a close friend of the Obama family said in an interview for this book. "That's Valerie's opinion: he's eager to recapture the freedom of his youth. He sees himself as sort of a hipster ex-president, a cool guy. He wants to go back in terms of fashion and style and his days as a leader of the Choom Gang in Hawaii."

In his pot-smoking days at the Punahou School in Honolulu, Obama was a member of a group that went by the nickname "the Choom Gang." Choom is a variation of the word "chum," or close friend, but Obama's pals used it as slang for smoking marijuana.

Despite stories that Obama had quit smoking upon entering the White House, he had never kicked his cigarette habit, and as soon as he was free of the responsibilities of the presidency, he went back to smoking marijuana.

"He smokes weed once or twice a week," said the close family friend. "He stopped while he was president, because he knew that it impaired his judgment, but he feels he can get away with it now, so why not? He likes it, and quite a few of his friends do it fairly regularly.

"He gets the weed from friends who visit him," the source continued. "Many of them are from his Chicago days. He doesn't buy it himself.

"I was told he keeps a small stash in his bedroom. [The former president and first lady have separate bedrooms in their mansion in the Kalorama section of Washington, DC.] He has rolling papers and knows how to roll a joint. Sometimes he'll smoke in his bedroom, and sometimes in the back yard. But mostly he does it when he's traveling.

"At one point, he became concerned about people smelling pot around Kalorama and asked friends to get him some edible stuff. They got him brownies, cookies, and gummy bears infused with THC [the chemical compound in cannabis].

"He had a blow up with Michelle when Malia was caught on video smoking what looked like a joint at a Lollapalooza concert in Chicago. When the tape of Malia went viral, Michelle blew up at him; she said it was his fault because he set a bad example for his daughters, that it was OK to use pot.

"Barack tried to brush off the whole thing, which only made Michelle more furious. She started yelling at him so loudly that the maids could hear. That made Barack furious; he can't stand being yelled at; his mother had a temper and a shrill voice. So he walked out on Michelle and slammed the door behind him."

■ ■ ■

Obama yearned to travel in his post-presidency, and he had his heart set on Tetiaroa, the island in French Polynesia that Marlon Brando called paradise.

In 1967, after shooting *Mutiny on the Bounty*, Brando bought the atoll of Tetiaroa as his private getaway. Now, fifty years later, Obama staged what might be called a mutiny of his own: he refused to heed the pleas of his party to set up a shadow government and undermine his successor in the White House. Instead, he asked aides who handled his travel and the Secret Service to make arrangements for a trip to French Polynesia. In March, he flew off by himself to Honolulu in a Gulfstream, then to Fa'a'ā airport in Tahiti, and then on a prop to Tetiaroa.

At The Brando, the luxury, eco-resort on Tetiaroa, he stayed at a villa with its own plunge pool, private beach, and TV media room. He snorkeled; rode bikes, outriggers, and canoes; sampled the French cuisine at Les Mutinés restaurant; watched the sun set from Bob's Bar; and refused to take phone calls from anyone except Michelle and Valerie Jarrett.

It seemed fitting that Obama would end up on Brando's island, since the two men had much in common.

Brando was considered one of the greatest movie actors of all time—and yet he hated being an actor. Obama was considered one of the most compelling political campaigners of all time—and yet he hated being a politician.

The movie critic Pauline Kael once labeled Brando "the rebel." Obama, when asked to pick his favorite character from *Star Wars*, chose Han Solo, because he's "a little bit of a rebel."

Brando was a leftwing activist who participated in the civil rights and Native American protest movements. Obama was a leftwing community organizer who became the most liberal president in American history.

Brando was a famous recluse. Obama was famous for preferring his own company to that of others.

■ ■ ■

Valerie Jarrett pleaded with him not to go. She wanted him to stay in Washington and answer the call of his demoralized party. She argued that in the wake of Hillary's defeat, there was no one in the party—not Nancy Pelosi, not Chuck Schumer, not Bernie Sanders, not Elizabeth Warren—who had Obama's political muscle. The machinery was already in place: Organizing for Action, a nonprofit spinoff of Obama's two successful presidential campaigns, had 32,000 trained volunteers across the country "ready to roll."

But after eight years in the White House, Obama was burned out. During a conference call with his distraught supporters a week after the election, his only words of consolation were, "Don't mope. And don't get complacent."

"Barack had no intention after he left the White House of dealing with union leaders and politicians and the whole mess of the resistance to Trump," the Obama family friend said. "This isn't how he saw himself. His role model was Teddy Roosevelt, who was fifty-one when he left the White House. [Obama was fifty-five.] He wanted to have adventures, explore Africa and South America, and write books about his explorations. He'd sooner have died than turn into Jimmy Carter in baggy farmer's jeans hammering nails into buildings."

It was well known in Washington that Obama hated the day-to-day scrum of politics. When he was running for a second presidential term, Bob Schieffer, then the anchor of CBS' *Face the Nation*, asked him about his aversion to politics.

"Do you like politicians?" Schieffer asked. "Do you like politics? Do you like this job?"

Obama couldn't come up with a convincing answer.

Like many liberals, he loved humanity in the abstract, but didn't care for individual people.

"Obama doesn't really have the joy of the game," said Larry Summers, the former director of Obama's national economic council. "Clinton basically loved negotiating with a bunch of pols, about anything. Whereas Obama, he really didn't like these guys.... I don't think anybody has a sense of his deep feelings about things. I don't think anybody has a sense of his deep feelings about people."

While I was researching *The Amateur*, my 2012 bestseller on Obama, his old friends in Chicago and several of his donors complained to me about Obama's attitude of indifference. He didn't answer their phone calls; he never invited them to the White House; he only seemed to care for Michelle, their daughters, Valerie Jarrett—and himself.

■　■　■

Over the past twenty-six years, Jarrett had played a vital role in Obama's life. She served as his marriage counselor when his relationship with Michelle appeared to founder; she got rid of an attractive female campaign worker who made Michelle jealous; she lined up support for Obama with liberal activists, pro-choice women, gays and lesbians, wealthy donors, and leaders of the African-American community; she hosted the Obamas at her home in Oak Bluffs, the traditional summer residence on Martha's Vineyard for prosperous African-Americans; she served as Obama's most effective public advocate ("I think Barack knew that he had God-given talents that were extraordinary," she told *The New Yorker* editor David Remnick); she held Obama's hand when he expressed a lack of confidence in his chance of wresting the Democratic nomination from Hillary Clinton; she stiffened Obama's resolve when, as president, he failed to promote the leftwing causes and policies that helped get him elected; and she defended Obama from the criticism that he was ungrateful to his supporters and political colleagues ("He doesn't feel the need to thank his friends").

But while doing all this for Obama (and, just as important, for her best friend Michelle), Jarrett came in for criticism of her own. In a widely read piece in *Politico*, Carol Felsenthal, a columnist for *Chicago Magazine*, recommended that President Obama fire Valerie Jarrett.

"Jarrett," wrote Felsenthal, "micromanages guest lists…hangs out in the private quarters and often joins the Obamas for dinner. [Jarrett] seems to isolate [Obama[from the people who might help him."

"A *New Republic* profile of Jarrett by Noam Scheiber emphasized 'Jarrett's obsessiveness about control,'" David Garrow wrote in his exhaustive biography of Obama, *Rising Star: The Making of Barack Obama*. "The piece described how Jarrett rebuffed helpful criticism. 'She just cuts it off. It's stone cold,' one source told Scheiber, who thought Jarrett was as responsible as anyone for how 'Obama has become even more persuaded of his righteousness as the years have gone on.'"

In her defense, Jarrett often had to push Obama to pay attention to his job as president and do the expedient political thing. A big part of the problem, Jarrett confided to friends, was Obama's laziness.

Obama didn't dispute Jarrett's characterization of him. "I think there's a laziness in me," he once admitted. "It's probably from, you know, growing up in Hawaii and it's sunny outside, and sitting on the beach."

From long experience, Jarrett had learned how to deal with Obama's quirks; she simply presented him with a fait accompli. And so, as he reached the end of his second term in the White House, she decided— with Michelle's concurrence—that the Obama family would remain in the nation's capital. No president since Woodrow Wilson, who was incapacitated by a stroke, had done that. Jarrett came up with a convenient excuse: the Obamas had to stick around until their younger daughter, Sasha, graduated from the exclusive Sidwell Friends School.

Several months before the Obamas left the White House, Jarrett and Michelle went house hunting in Washington. They found a large home in the fashionable Kalorama section, just two miles from the White House, and they rented it for a reported $22,000 a month from Joe Lockhart, a former press secretary to Bill Clinton who was now the top communications official for the National Football League.[1]

The 6,441-square-foot house had nine bedrooms, one of which was reserved for Jarrett. To decorate the Kalorama house, Michelle hired Michael S. Smith, a Los Angeles-based interior designer who had decorated several rooms in the White House during the Obamas' residence. In the Obamas' new living room, Smith hung blue and white floor-length draperies that wouldn't have looked out of place in the White House.

Obama quickly made himself at home in Kalorama. At night after dinner, he often retreated to his study, where he played with his favorite new video games—Styx: Shards of Darkness, Tom Clancy's Ghost Recon, and Halo War 2 Ultimate Edition. And smoked weed.

■ ■ ■

In April, after several weeks of living apart, Michelle joined her husband at The Brando. They then boarded David Geffen's $300 million yacht, and sailed the Pacific with Geffen's other A-list guests—Oprah Winfrey, Tom Hanks, and Bruce Springsteen.

"A snapshot of the former president taking a picture of Michelle on the deck of Mr. Geffen's yacht, the Rising Sun, went viral on the Internet," reported the *New York Times*' Michael D. Shear.

Obama made sure that no photos were taken of him smoking marijuana while on Geffen's yacht.

The Obamas arrived home in late April just as Donald Trump was nearing the end of his tumultuous first hundred days.

The new president had signed twenty-four executive orders, twenty-two memorandums, and twenty proclamations; ordered a missile strike on Syria and a ban on immigration from seven predominantly Muslim countries; successfully shepherded the Supreme Court nomination of Neil Gorsuch through the Senate, and failed to shepherd a bill through the House of Representatives to repeal and replace Obamacare; withdrew the United States from the Trans-Pacific Partnership; approved the Keystone and Dakota Access pipelines; fired his national security adviser, Michael Flynn; promised to scrap Obama's Clean Power Plan and abandon the Paris Climate Accord; and accused Obama of wiretapping him.

The partisan mood in the country was toxic. Enraged Democrats were more determined than ever to impeach Trump or run him out of office using the Twenty-Fifth Amendment. It had become the Democrats' overriding obsession.

But where was Obama?

Why didn't he speak up?

"Why are we not hearing from him?" said Sarah Kovner, a wealthy liberal New York activist and donor. "Democrats are desperate. Everything that Trump is doing really requires a response."

Before Obama had a chance to unpack from his trip, Jarrett sat him down for a talk. She told him that David Axelrod, the architect of Obama's two successful runs for the White House, agreed with her that if Obama wanted to save his legacy, he had to become the heart and soul of the resistance movement.

But Obama was in no mood to listen. He came up with a ton of excuses: he had to get started writing his White House memoirs, (for which he had been paid an advance of $60 million); he had to deliver a speech at the Kennedy Library, where he was being honored as the 2017 recipient of the Profile in Courage Award; he had to give two other speeches, for which he was being paid $400,000 apiece—one at a health care luncheon sponsored by the Cantor Fitzgerald investment bank, and another to advertisers of the A&E cable network.

Jarrett was an old hand at dealing with Obama's stubborn nature, and she went to work on him. What about that Muslim ban? Was Barack going to stand for that? And how about those Dreamers, the kids who were brought here illegally as minors and whom Trump was threatening to deport? And Obamacare? And the Iran nuclear deal? And the Paris Climate Accord? And Michelle's school lunch nutrition guidelines, about which she felt so passionate? Didn't he care how his wife felt?

And she didn't stop there.

Jarrett arranged a visit by Hillary Clinton, who urged Obama to join her in leading the resistance.

Jarrett made sure that Obama received assurances of support from George Soros, who had been funding Obama since his early days in the Illinois state legislature. Soros promised that he'd put together a war chest with the help of other liberal moneybags such as investment banker David Shaw, real estate heiress Amy Goldman Fowler, venture capitalists Ryan Smith and Kenneth Levine, San Francisco-based philanthropists John and Marcia Goldman, medical device heir Jon Stryker, and real estate investors Wayne Jordan and Mary Quinn Delaney.

Jarrett persuaded the Obamas to buy the Kalorama mansion for $8.1 million, thereby advancing her political agenda of making the former president a force in Washington for years to come.

But it was all to no avail.

"Valerie says Barack is listless," said the Obama family friend. "He mostly sits in his study in the Kalorama house playing video games. He's behind writing on his memoirs. He isn't terribly enthused about the book right now, and he hasn't done a lick of work on it. He'll take phone calls from show business friends like Bruce Springsteen, Jay-Z, and Tom Hanks, but he refuses to talk politics.

"Michelle invites activists like Black Lives Matter people to Kalorama in the hope that Barack will get engaged," the friend continued, "but he suddenly remembers that he has to be somewhere and he'll go out and take a walk.

"He continues to wave off most calls, including from Chuck Schumer and Elizabeth Warren, but when [Democrat Senator] Cory Booker called, Barack jumped at the chance to take it. Booker's preparing legislation to legalize marijuana on the federal level so that African Americans and other low-income people aren't disproportionately jailed for marijuana offenses. Barack was on board right away. That's the first and only time he seemed animated about politics since he left the White House.

"Come the mid-term elections in 2018, he'll give some speeches, but as far as leading the resistance to Trump is concerned, he's not interested. He hates being in D.C. The two women forced it upon him, and he's cranky and angry about that. He'd rather be traveling. He doesn't want to turn Kalorama into the headquarters of a shadow government.

"Valerie thinks that she and Michelle will eventually motivate him to snap out of his fog. They've always been able to do that in the past.

"But frankly, knowing Barack for as long as I do, I think what you see is what you're going to get."

27

THE EYE OF THE STORM

I t was February 12—twenty-three days into the new Trump administration—and Michael Flynn, the national security adviser, was in
trouble. Transcripts of his conversations with Russian Ambassador
Sergey Kislyak, which had been leaked to the press, revealed that Flynn
had misled Vice President Mike Pence and other White House officials
about the subject of his phone calls with the Russians.

The mainstream media were feasting on the story, which portrayed
the Trump White House in chaos. But no one was happier about Flynn's
imminent political demise than Barack Obama's old friend and campaign
guru David Axelrod.

"I got a call from Axelrod the night before the White House
announced Flynn's forced resignation," said a prominent Democratic
Party operative who was interviewed for this book. "He told me, 'This
isn't about Flynn; this is about getting Trump out.' He said that if the
Dems could prove that Trump ordered Flynn to promise the Russians

relief from sanctions, it could be an impeachable offense. 'That's our hope,' Axelrod said."

■ ■ ■

If Axelrod was pinning his hopes on exposing a secret plot between Mike Flynn and Sergey Kislyak, he was in for a big disappointment. The portly, sixty-six-year-old Kislyak, who was nearing retirement, had served as Moscow's ambassador since 2008, and he was a familiar figure at Washington cocktail parties and other political gatherings (with the approval of the Obama State Department, he attended the 2016 Republican National Convention in Cleveland). Kislyak had met with practically everyone on the State Department's Russian Desk, dozens of members of the United States Senate, and the chairmen and ranking members of key committees in the House of Representatives. During that time, his phone was routinely tapped, and no one in the U.S. intelligence community ever mistook him for a spy.

"Like most ambassadors in these days of easy and instant communication," said an ambassador from the Middle East, "Kislyak is nothing more than a messenger boy for his boss, the foreign minister."

On December 28, three weeks before Trump took office, Kislyak was summoned to the State Department and informed that the United States was expelling thirty-five Russian diplomats and imposing new sanctions on Moscow in retaliation for Russia's meddling in the U.S. presidential election. That same day, Mike Flynn, in his position as Trump's chief adviser on national security affairs, called Kislyak and urged him to send a message to the Kremlin: *Don't retaliate in kind for the expulsion. Wait for Trump to take office.*

Flynn did not promise Kislyak anything in this initial conversation, and four days later, on January 2, the Russian ambassador called him back to continue their discussion. The intercept of their conversations was duly recorded by the FBI.

There the matter would have rested, except for one thing: thanks to the FISA warrant obtained back in October by Sally Yates, the deputy attorney general, Flynn was a target of the FBI's investigation into suspected collusion between the Trump campaign and the Russians.

As an American citizen, Flynn's identity was supposed to be "masked," or protected from exposure. However, Susan Rice had made sure that the names of Trump associates scooped up in intercepts would be unmasked and disseminated widely throughout the intelligence community, assuring that they would be leaked to the press.

And that's exactly what happened.

"The *New York Times* and the *Washington Post* reported that the transcript of the phone call reviewed over the weekend by the White House could be read different ways," wrote *Bloomberg News'* Eli Lake. "One White House official with knowledge of the conversations told me that the Russian ambassador raised the sanctions to Flynn and that Flynn responded that the Trump team would be taking office in a few weeks and would review Russian policy and sanctions. That's neither illegal nor improper.

"This is what police states do," Lake continued. "In the past, it was considered scandalous for senior U.S. officials to even request the identities of U.S officials incidentally monitored by the government (normally they are redacted from intelligence reports). John Bolton's nomination to be the U.S. ambassador to the United Nations was derailed in 2006 after the NSA confirmed he had made ten such requests when he was undersecretary of state for arms control in George W. Bush's first term."

Representative David Nunes, the Republican chairman of the House Permanent Select Committee on Intelligence, agreed with Lake.

"There does appear to be a well-orchestrated effort to attack Flynn and others in the [Trump] administration," Nunes said. "From the leaking of phone calls between the president and foreign leaders to what appears to be high-level FISA Court information, to the leaking of American citizens being denied security clearances, it looks like a pattern.... First it's Flynn, next it will be Kellyanne Conway, then it will be Steve Bannon, then it will be Reince Priebus."

Nunes' suspicions of an orchestrated attack were corroborated on January 26—six days after Trump assumed office—when Sally Yates paid a visit to the White House, and warned that Mike Flynn had been "compromised." According to Yates, Flynn's failure to tell Vice President Mike Pence that sanctions had been discussed with Kislyak left Flynn open to blackmail.

"That created a compromise situation," Yates later told Congress, "a situation where the national security adviser could be blackmailed by the Russians."[1]

"Nonsense," said Michael Rubin, a resident scholar at the American Enterprise Institute. "Adversaries blackmail American officials for financial, criminal, and sexual improprieties, not because someone lied in Washington."

■ ■ ■

The firing of Lieutenant General Michael Flynn was a major victory for the villains in the resistance movement. In the words of Eli Lake, Flynn was "a fat target." As the former director of the Defense Intelligence Agency, Flynn was a fierce critic of the CIA, which he blamed for failing to foresee the rise of the Islamic State. He was also someone Trump liked and whose opinions he respected.

"Flynn warned [as far back as 2014] that the United States was actually less safe from the threat of terrorism…than it was prior to the 9/11 attacks," wrote *Politico's* James Kitfield. "In remarkably blunt comments for a general still in uniform, Flynn admitted to feeling like a lone voice inside an Obama administration that seemed to believe that the 2011 death of Osama bin Laden had signaled the end of radical Islamic terrorism as a seminal threat."

In a dramatic speech at the Republican National Convention, Flynn attacked Barack Obama as a "weak and spineless" leader whose "fumbling indecisiveness," "willful ignorance," and "total incompetence" were responsible for the spread of terrorism throughout the western world.

It was only a matter of time before the U.S. intelligence community and the Obama holdovers in the Deep State retaliated against Flynn. In a flurry of leaks, stories began appearing in the *Washington Post* and other newspapers that Flynn had visited Moscow, where he sat next to

Vladimir Putin at a dinner and received payments for a speech to RT, the Kremlin's propaganda TV network. When those charges faded from public attention, a new series of leaks charged that Flynn had worked as a lobbyist for a Turkish energy and mining company that had ties to the Kremlin.

The Flynn imbroglio was at the heart of a storm that engulfed the Trump administration. But even some of Flynn's toughest critics were concerned about the way he was brought down.

"The whole episode is evidence of the precipitous and ongoing collapse of America's democratic institutions—not a sign of their resiliency," wrote Damon Linker, a senior correspondent at theweek.com. "Flynn's ouster was a soft coup (or political assassination) engineered by anonymous intelligence community bureaucrats. Far too many Trump critics appear not to care that these intelligence agents leaked highly sensitive information to the press—mostly because Trump critics are pleased with the result," Linker continued. "...I have no interest in defending Flynn [but] no matter what Flynn did, it is simply not the role of the Deep State to target a man working in one of the political branches of the government by dishing to reporters about information it has gathered clandestinely."

28

A BREACH OF PUBLIC TRUST

O n February 27, the day before he was to deliver a speech to a joint session of Congress, Donald Trump appeared on *Fox and Friends*. He hadn't been tweeting much lately—he seemed to be saving his ammunition for the big speech—but when he was asked if he believed Barack Obama was helping organize the street demonstrations, town hall protests, and leaks that were undermining his administration, he couldn't help doing what came naturally—speak his mind.

"I think that President Obama is behind it because his people [are] certainly behind it," he said. "And some of the leaks possibly come from that group."

The group that Trump referred to, Organizing for Action, was the spin-off from Obama's two presidential campaigns, and was staffed mostly by former Obama officials. They were, as Trump suspected, a major power behind the "resistance" movement, and a source of many of the anti-Trump leaks. Trump, however, was mistaken if he thought that Obama himself took a direct role in the "resistance." Despite the efforts of his former staff, Valerie Jarrett, and his wife, Obama demonstrated little interest in setting up a shadow government at his home in the Kalorama section of Washington, DC.

"Valerie tried to engage Barack in the resistance, but he only gave her an hour here and an hour there of his attention,"[1] a source familiar with Obama's post-presidential life said in an interview for this book. "Barack's enjoying his life as a private citizen, and it's hard to say he doesn't deserve to. He shoots hoops with a neighbor, plays a bunch of video games, and has ordered a hip new wardrobe, including a leather jacket and $300 Prada sunglasses.

"Meanwhile, Valerie's been getting involved with Indivisible and the other resistance groups," the source continued. "She's enlisted the help of [former deputy national security adviser] Ben Rhodes, who helped Obama pull off the Iran nuclear deal. Other Obama people are working on union leaders, especially [Richard] Trumka [the president of the AFL-CIO], who isn't completely committed to the resistance, because Trump's trillion-dollar infrastructure plans translate into tens of thousands of union jobs.

"As the midterm elections draw closer, Valerie and Ben intend to set up venues for Barack to make occasional speeches. He'll defend his legacy, and show the contrast between his cool personality and Trump's jagged edges. But he's not going to take personal shots at Trump. He intends to stay above the fray."[2]

■ ■ ■

On the eve of Trump's address to Congress, the villains in Organizing for Action and the Deep State—mostly former Obama officials who were embedded in government agencies throughout Washington—fired off a series of leaks to their favorite reporters. Their aim was to use the so-called Russian collusion story to eclipse the media coverage of Trump's speech. And their gambit worked. For the next several days, newspapers and TV networks indulged in an orgy of anti-Trump stories.

- The *New York Times*: "American allies, including the British and Dutch, provided information describing meetings in European cities between Russian officials—and others close to Russia's president, Vladimir Putin—and associates of President-elect Trump."
- The *Washington Post*: "Then-Senator Jeff Sessions (R–Ala.) spoke twice last year with Russia's ambassador to the United States, Justice Department officials said, encounters he did not disclose when asked about possible contacts between members of President Trump's campaign and representatives of Moscow during Sessions' confirmation hearing to become attorney general."

The stories, which were based on unreliable and anonymous sources, were full of sound and fury and signified nothing (Sessions' contacts with Russia's ambassador, for instance, had nothing to do with the campaign, but were simply part of the everyday life of a U.S. senator who attended public events and had meetings with more than two dozen ambassadors over the course of the previous year.) But they enraged Trump. He doubled down on his attacks on Obama and went further than ever before. He accused the former president of tapping his phone, and called him "sick."

@realDonaldTrump

How low has President Obama gone to "tapp" my phones during the very sacred election process. This is Nixon/Watergate. Bad (or sick) guy!

4:02 AM—4 March 2017

■ ■ ■

The day after Trump's jaw-dropping tweet against the former president, Barack Obama was in his home office, searching online for designer jeans at fredsegal.com. Valerie Jarrett interrupted his shopping spree to inform him that James Clapper, the former director of national intelligence, was on the phone and needed to speak to him urgently. That morning—Sunday, March 5—Clapper had been interviewed by Chuck Todd on *Meet the Press*, and tried to debunk Donald Trump's charge that Obama had ordered the wiretapping of Trump Tower during the recent election campaign.

"There was no such wiretap activity mounted against the president, the president-elect, at the time, or as a candidate, or against his campaign," Clapper told Todd.

Clapper didn't stop there. Under questioning by Todd, he also denied that there had ever been a FISA Court order giving the intelligence community permission to conduct surveillance of Trump and his associates.

Both of those statements were false, which wasn't surprising, given Clapper's history of lying. He had perjured himself several years before when he testified under oath to the Senate Intelligence Committee that the NSA never monitored the phone calls and emails of American citizens.

"Unfortunately for Clapper," radio host Laura Ingraham pointed out, "Edward Snowden's purloined information was made public and it was revealed that [Clapper was] a shameless, conscienceless liar. Because the NSA was actually doing exactly [that]."

What's more, the *New York Times* had run a front-page story back in January—six days before Trump's inauguration—confirming Trump's subsequent wiretapping charge. The headline: "Wiretapped Data Used in Inquiry of Trump Aides."

"One official," reported the *Times*, "said intelligence reports based on some of the wiretapped communications had been provided to the [Obama] White House."

Of course, Obama knew about the FISA warrant, because he had given Susan Rice the nod to unmask the names of Trump campaign associates scooped up in FISA-approved intelligence intercepts.

"The president wasn't happy with the phone conversation [with Clapper], and at one point he had enough," said a source close to Valerie Jarrett, who spoke on background in an interview for this book. "Valerie said he looked at his watch and made a gesture cutting his throat, a sign that the conversation was over.

"This was exactly what Michelle had warned him about last Christmas," the source continued. "The Trump-Russian collusion story was coming back to 'bite him in the ass.'"

■   ■   ■

The mainstream media didn't see it that way. They dismissed Trump's wiretapping charge as yet another example of the tweet-happy president's addiction to "exaggeration" and "lies."

"Trump offered no citations nor did he point to any credible news report to back up his accusations," wrote the *Washington Post*, which ironically didn't have any credible citations of its own, or make any effort to get them.

"A cardinal rule of the Obama administration was that no White House official ever conferred with any independent investigation led by the Department of Justice," said Kevin Lewis, a spokesman for Obama.

That, too, was demonstrably false.

As I reported in *Guilty as Sin*, then-Attorney General Loretta Lynch violated the Department of Justice's ethical rules and regularly briefed Valerie Jarrett on the FBI's investigation of Hillary's use of a private email server.

"Trump was definitely onto something about the wiretaps," Tom Fitton, the president of Judicial Watch, told the author of this book. "Ben Rhodes and other Obama advisers were tracking and reviewing intelligence reports on Trump and his people. This was part of a movement to remove Trump from office before the next presidential election, and in the meantime to make it nearly impossible for him to get his people appointed. It forced him to rely on career civil servants who are hostile to him. He still has all these former Obama people running top jobs at the Department of Justice."

Christopher Farrell, the director of investigations and research at Judicial Watch, added another perspective.

"When you talk about Trump, you've got to remember that despite his great wealth, he's still a guy from Queens," Farrell told me. "So when Trump says 'Obama wiretapped my phones,' let me translate that from Queens. It means 'Obama and his operatives leaked classified information from clandestine surveillance against me and my team.'"

■ ■ ■

Final vindication of Trump's wiretap charge came in early April. According to former U.S. Attorney Joseph diGenova, Susan Rice and her deputy, Ben Rhodes, requested that the National Security Council, the Department of Defense, the director of national intelligence, and the director of the CIA produce "detailed spreadsheets" of intercepted phone calls involving Trump and his aides. The spreadsheets provided a roadmap for the anti-Trump forces in the intelligence community and led directly to a burst of new leaks.

"This was a stream of information that was supposed to be hermetically sealed from politics, [but] the Obama administration found a way to blow a hole in that wall," said Michael Doran, a former senior director at the National Security Council. "This is leaking of signal intelligence. That's a felony. And you can get ten years for that. It's a tremendous abuse of the system. We're not supposed to be monitoring American citizens. Bigger than the crime is the breach of public trust."

29

COMPLICITY

Who leaked all those damaging stories about Donald Trump to the media?

Reliable reporting on this subject was scarce to the point of nonexistent. The liberal media was generally quiet on the subject. Newspapers and TV news divisions had little incentive to expose the leakers, because sensational stories based on those leaks were good for business—they translated into increased circulation, ratings, and advertising revenue.

Only one leaker had been arrested and charged with violating the law—a twenty-five-year-old Air Force veteran and Bernie Sanders supporter named Reality Winner. With no one else being held responsible, the leaks kept coming.

Even the Oval Office wasn't immune. "A day after firing FBI Director James Comey, Trump met with Russian Foreign Minister Sergey Lavrov and Russian Ambassador Sergey Kislyak in the Oval Office,"

174 ALL OUT WAR

noted Jonathan Easley in *The Hill.* "Three of Trump's most trusted advisers were present—Secretary of State Rex Tillerson, national security adviser H.R. McMaster and deputy national security adviser Dina Powell.... And yet out of that small group, damaging and highly specific details attributed to U.S. government officials spilled on to the pages [of] the *Washington Post* and the *New York Times* [that] Trump had revealed sensitive information to the Russians about an ISIS plot that Israeli officials had asked him to keep secret."

A report released by Ron Johnson, the chairman of the Senate Homeland Security and Government Affairs Committee, said that "under President Trump, leaks are flowing at the rate of one a day. Articles published by a range of national news organizations between January 20 and May 25, 2017, included at least 125 stories with leaked information potentially damaging to national security.... [Leaks] of comparable information during the Trump administration [were] about seven times higher than the same period during the two previous administrations."

"The Trump leaks show the sweeping nature of this enterprise, coming as they have from 'U.S. officials,' 'former U.S. officials,' 'senior U.S. officials,' 'intelligence officials,' 'Justice Department officials,' 'defense officials,' and 'law-enforcement officials,'" noted Kimberley A. Strassel, a columnist with the *Wall Street Journal.* "One story cited more than two dozen anonymous sources. Alarmingly, the titles and the nature of the information disclosed, indicate that many leaks are coming directly from the U.S. intelligence community."

The effort to identify leakers was complicated by the fact that the pool of potential leakers was so vast. President Obama had lowered the classification of sensitive electronic intercepts targeting the Trump campaign, thereby allowing hundreds, if not thousands, of people in the government to obtain access to potentially defamatory information.

"Investigations, usually from the FBI, will determine who in the first place had access to the leaked information," said Steven Aftergood, a government secrecy specialist with the Federation of American Scientists. "If it's a very large number, that might be the end of the matter because it might simply be too hard to narrow it down through ordinary investigative techniques."

■ ■ ■

Based on my reporting, I would point to four people as prime suspects in what might be called "Leakgate."

John Brennan. The first, and perhaps most obvious, was former CIA Director John Brennan, the most politicized member of the Obama administration's intelligence community, and a known Trump hater. During the final months of the presidential campaign, Brennan briefed Obama on an almost-daily basis on the alleged collusion between Trump and his associates and the Russians. Brennan used the unverified (and discredited) anti-Trump dossier, which had been slapped together by a British spy, as a device to drive the investigation, and he gave Obama a national security rationale to double down on his effort to discredit Trump and help Hillary win the White House.

Trump replaced Brennan as head of the CIA with former Congressman Mike Pompeo, but the holdovers from the Brennan regime continued their dirty work. They were particularly opposed to Trump's policy of seeking areas of common interest with Russia, including the fight against Islamic terrorism, and a ceasefire in the Syrian civil war. Despite Pompeo's best efforts to control the vast CIA bureaucracy, the agency became a fount of leaks aimed at delegitimizing the new president.

Carl Ghattas. A second suspect was the National Security Branch of the FBI run by Carl Ghattas. Representative Jason Chaffetz, the chairman of the House Oversight Committee, and Representative Bob Goodlatte, the chairman of the House Judiciary Committee, suspected that Ghattas' branch was the source of many leaks. They sent a letter to the inspector general of the Department of Justice requesting "that your office begin an immediate investigation into whether classified information was mishandled here."

Samantha Power. A third suspect was Samantha Power, the ambassador to the United Nations and an idol of the left wing of the Democratic

Party. Unlike Brennan and Ghattas, Power had no official connection to the intelligence community, and therefore no compelling interest to request permission to unmask the identities of Americans "incidentally" intercepted by the FBI or the NSA. And yet she made hundreds of such requests, which gave her team at the UN ammunition to use in leaks against Trump.

Hillary Clinton. A fourth suspect was Hillary Clinton. According to my sources in the White House and the Justice Department, Valerie Jarrett secretly briefed Hillary during the presidential campaign on the FISA Court warrants that targeted Trump and his associates. Jarrett worked hand in glove with national security adviser Susan Rice, who revealed to Hillary the identity of the Trump people she had unmasked and the specific nature of their alleged connections to the Russians. With this information in hand, my sources said, the members of Hillary's infamous war room—David Brock, Philippe Reines, and Sidney Blumenthal—went to work leaking those names to the media.

■ ■ ■

"By making Hillary complicit in his schemes against Trump, Obama put her in serious legal jeopardy," said one of Bill Clinton's most trusted legal advisers in an interview for this book. "She became legally entangled in the multiple Russian investigations.

"You always have to assume that any communication you have with someone in the White House is logged in, and that the content of your conversation is duly noted," he added. "That information can be subpoenaed and wind up in the hands of congressional investigators and the FBI.

"If Hillary was asked under oath about her conversations with Valerie Jarrett and Susan Rice, she'd have to report them accurately or perjure herself. And if her former campaign people and members of her so-called war room were asked under oath if they leaked the unmasked names to the media, they'd perjure themselves and go to jail if they were caught lying.

"I was so worried about all this that I asked a friend, a retired FISA Court judge, who was highly informed on the matter, to fly down to the Clinton Library [in Little Rock] to brief Bill on Hillary's exposure. Bill sent a Gulfstream to Washington to get him.

"He and Bill hit it off right away. Bill was his charming self, and invited the judge to join him in chipping golf balls off the roof of his penthouse. They sipped beer and had a great time.

"Later in the afternoon, they had a serious conversation in Bill's office about Hillary's legal exposure. The judge said that merely having knowledge of what Obama, Jarrett, and Rice were up to could cause Hillary a legal headache. If she knew that a sitting president was using the intelligence community for political purposes, and she tacitly approved his strategy, or didn't say anything to stop him, that could get her into hot water. He said that Hillary should think back to the campaign and whether she said anything compromising when she met Jarrett and Rice. And he said Hillary would be well-advised to make notes about what she knew and when she knew it, in case she was called upon to testify.

"Once their talk was over, the party began. About a dozen young women were escorted up to the penthouse. Many were quite young, in their early twenties, but others were a bit older. They were women Bill meets regularly in Little Rock. They were obviously delighted to be invited to Bill's penthouse and to be in the former president's company. Some I recognized from other parties that I had attended up there.

"As always, Bill had the library's restaurant cater the party. The chefs used the herbs that are grown on his rooftop garden. It was southern food, the kind Bill grew up eating, and the dishes he and Hillary served when he was governor of Arkansas. Cornmeal crusted pork loin with green tomato salsa; fried chicken with hot buffalo sauce; fried tortillas with black beans; and *queso blanco* topped with a fried egg.

"The bar was stocked with Johnny Walker Blue Label, which is Bill's favorite scotch. The judge flirted with the women and had a great old time. Who wouldn't? It's like visiting fantasy land."

30

TWEET STORMS

"I think that maybe I wouldn't be here if it wasn't for Twitter," Donald Trump told Tucker Carlson of Fox News.

Trump's love affair with Twitter was not something new: he had been tweeting long before he ran for president. His first tweet was posted on May 4, 2009; it plugged his upcoming appearance on *The Late Show with David Letterman*. Since then, his tweets had become more and more combative. When it came to his enemies, he believed in the doctrine of massive retaliation: he hit them back ten times harder than they hit him.

During the presidential campaign, Trump said he wasn't ready to act presidential "quite yet," but that at some point "I'm going to be so presidential that you people will be so bored, and I will come back as a presidential person."

That didn't happen. His tweets continued to be classic Trump—brazen and disrespectful and unpresidential. And he wasn't the least bit apologetic about them. In fact, he thought they were right on the mark.

"My use of social media is not Presidential—it's MODERN DAY PRESIDENTIAL," he tweeted.

His tweets drove the media crazy. He was widely condemned for criticizing women for their looks (Arianna Huffington, Carly Fiorina, Ted Cruz's wife Heidi, and Mika Brzezinski).

He was taken to task for undercutting his own Justice Department attorneys, who argued that his immigration policy was not a travel ban ("That's right," he tweeted, "we need a TRAVEL BAN for certain DANGEROUS countries, not some politically correct term that won't help us protect our people").

And he was faulted for stooping to attack knee-jerk Hollywood liberals ("Meryl Streep, one of the most over-rated actresses in Hollywood, doesn't know me but attacked last night at the Golden Globes," he tweeted. "She is a Hillary flunky who lost big").

As he reached the April 29 date of his first hundred days, even some of his supporters expressed qualms about his incendiary tweets.

"The tweeting makes everybody crazy," said Tom Barrack, chairman of the real estate investment management company Colony NorthStar, who was a close Trump friend. "There's just no gain in doing it."

"The pt cannot be stressed enough that tweets on legal matters seriously undermine Admin agenda and POTUS—and those who support him, as I do, need to reinforce that pt and not be shy about it," tweeted lawyer George Conway, the husband of White House counselor Kellyanne Conway.

Chris Ruddy, the president of Newsmax.com and a frequent visitor to the White House, urged the president to appoint someone to vet his tweets before he sent them out.

"There's nothing wrong with the tweeting," Ruddy said, "but a backstop would be smart."

"Trump always doubles and triples down on his mistakes," a veteran Washington-based diplomat, who was on friendly terms with Trump, told me. "I've never seen a nation's leader do that before. Eventually, when he realizes he can't go any further, he somehow extricates himself from the predicament of his own making."

Ed Rollins, who managed Ronald Reagan's 1984 campaign, and was now running a pro-Trump Super PAC called Great America, had this to say when I interviewed him about Trump's tweet storms: "Some days, he's his own worst enemy. He should shut up. All that stuff gets in the way of the message."

■ ■ ■

The debate over Trump's tweets was a cottage industry for those who made their living lecturing people on what they should think about the president. Much of the analysis of Trump's use of Twitter bordered on psychobabble.

"I've been covering Donald Trump off and on for more than 25 years," wrote Allan Sloan, a columnist for the *Washington Post*, "and what has always struck me is his lack of impulse control."

"Impulsive behavior is a matter of stakes; it represents the capacity in certain individuals to separate the outcomes of their choices from the process through which they decide to act in the first place," noted Timothy Denevi, an assistant professor at George Mason University and an expert on attention deficit disorder. "Trump during his unlikely success in both the Republican primary and the general election, relied on this exact type of disconnect to stymie his opponents. For Donald Trump, impulsivity is best described as a weaponized version of overreaction. He functions like a bared nerve, receiving and responding to stimuli in the same endless moment."

■ ■ ■

Not everyone thought Trump was on a self-destructive tear. In fact, several experts in the field of communications argued that when it came to the use of social media, Trump was a past master. He knew exactly what he was doing.

"One of the beautiful things about social media is it allows the conversation to seem very personal," said Karen North, director of the University of California Annenberg Digital Social Media Program. "In all honesty, love him or hate him, [Trump] has created a persona and a sense that he speaks to people directly. There is a desire and expectation for authentic communication. It can be seen by some people—instead of being inconsistent and raising problems of uncertainty—it can be seen as a guy who speaks the truth and doesn't care."

"A basic set of rules for surviving and thriving in the nation's capital—well understood by Washington veterans—would include: Don't make an enemy of the Federal Bureau of Investigation, keep potential enemies inside the tent and, above all, remember that it usually isn't the action, but the appearance of a cover-up that brings real trouble," wrote the *Wall Street Journal's* Gerald F. Seib. "Mr. Trump's supporters love the fact that he is the outsider willing to shatter the rules and norms that seem to govern life in Washington, so they likely aren't troubled—in fact, they likely will cheer."

Among the millions cheering was Cathy Accordino, a motor sport TV producer who was interviewed by the *Washington Times*. "He's showing us how to win again, how to take back our country," she said. "He's going in the face of these dissenting voices about his tweeting, facing them head on and saying, 'Excuse me, we're not going to do what you say anymore!'"

"In a word," said Frank Luntz, the Republican pollster and consultant, "[Trump's base] see him as their voice. And when their voice is shouted down, disrespected or simply ignored, that is an attack on them, not just an attack on Trump."

■ ■ ■

Trump's Twitter dustup with *Morning Joe's* co-host Mika Brzezinski outraged the elites on the East and West coasts, but was generally laughed off by his base in flyover country.

"I heard poorly rated @Morning Joe speaks badly of me (don't watch anymore)," he tweeted. "Then how come low I.Q. Mika, along with Psycho Joe, came to Mar-a-Lago 3 nights in a row around New Year's Eve and insisted on joining me. She was bleeding badly from a face-lift. I said no!"

The critics who slammed Trump for that tweet ignored the history of insults that had been directed at him on *Morning Joe*. For months, Brzezinski and Scarborough had been pushing Trump's buttons, describing him as certifiably insane and calling for his removal as president under the Twenty-Fifth Amendment. Donny Deutsch, a frequent *Morning Joe* guest, called Trump "physically disgusting to look at" and a "vulgar pig."

"They were attacking him and desperate to get a reaction from him," the Republican pollster John McLaughlin told me. "What they were really after wasn't Trump, it was higher ratings. Provoking an attack from the president worked, and *Morning Joe* beat *Fox and Friends* in ratings for the first time ever. The whole thing was concocted by Scarborough and his producers, and it was a cynical move."

PART FOUR

SIEGE

31

THE COMEY AFFAIR: PART I

Three days after Trump fired FBI Director James Comey, he posted a tweet that would have far-reaching political ramifications.

@realDonaldTrump

James Comey better hope that there are no "tapes" of our conversations before he starts leaking to the press!

8:26 AM—12 May 2017

Trump was responding to a story that was leaked to the *New York Times* by a close associate of Comey's. It described a private dinner between the president and the FBI director in which Trump supposedly asked Comey to pledge his loyalty to him—and Comey, who was portrayed as a straight arrow in the *Times*' article, refused. The story followed weeks of frenzied reports in the media—all of them based on anonymous sources—that Trump was a target of the FBI's Russian investigation.

The stories were untrue.

In fact, Comey had assured Trump on three occasions that he was not under investigation. Trump asked Comey to issue a public statement clearing him of suspicion—and once again the FBI director refused to accommodate the president's wishes.

Trump had every right—and plenty of reasons—to get rid of Comey. But it was a high-risk move. In the eighty-five years since Franklin Roosevelt occupied the White House, only one president, Bill Clinton, had removed the head of the FBI; he replaced William Sessions after the director had been accused of numerous ethical lapses. By firing Comey, Trump ignited a firestorm of protests, which ultimately resulted in the appointment of former FBI Director Robert Mueller as a special counsel investigating charges of the Kremlin's meddling in the presidential election and collusion between the Trump campaign and the Russians.

The villains in the Democratic Party and the media crowed; they said that Trump had made the biggest mistake of his political life. The specter of an unfettered investigation by a prosecutor who was beholden to no one, and who could endlessly expand the investigation, would loom over the White House for months to come, they said. But in order to assess the wisdom of Trump's action, and its potential fallout, you first had to know the true story behind the story.

■ ■ ■

According to my FBI sources, Trump and Comey started off on the right foot. Trump admired Comey's reputation as a tough prosecutor, and the FBI director viewed Trump as a pragmatic businessman who was used to delegating authority and giving people a free hand and a budget to do their job. Naturally, Comey had seen all the intelligence on the Trump campaign's contacts with Russian officials, and he had come to the conclusion, which he shared with his associates at the FBI, that Trump had done nothing legally wrong.

Furthermore, Comey agreed with Trump that the intelligence community was packed with Obama holdovers, and that the effort to delegitimize Trump had been designed in the White House by Valerie Jarrett and Susan Rice.

Comey never put much faith in the Obama White House. As far as he was concerned, Obama and his appointees frequently stepped over the ethical line. For instance, at Jarrett's urging, Attorney General Loretta Lynch asked Comey to call the FBI's criminal investigation of Hillary's emails "a matter," which was how the Clinton campaign liked to characterize the probe in order to make it sound innocuous.

Comey agreed to Lynch's request. Asked later why he went along with a blatant effort to misrepresent a criminal investigation, he came up with a lame excuse: "This [wasn't] a hill worthy dying on, and so I just said 'Okay.'"

The truth was, Comey was a shrewd political survivor, who always put his reputation ahead of every other consideration. He knew that the fix was in on the Hillary investigation. It was bad enough that Bill Clinton had met with Lynch while her plane sat on the tarmac at Phoenix airport. More damning was the fact that President Obama had done everything in his power to defend Hillary and her indefensible use of an unsecure and easily hackable email system.

"This," Obama told *60 Minutes*' Steve Kroft at the very beginning of the investigation, "is not a situation in which America's national security was endangered."

What Comey did not reveal in his subsequent testimony before Congress—and what I can report in this book—was that Obama privately tried on at least two occasions to influence the outcome of Comey's investigation of Hillary Clinton.

In early June 2016, according to my FBI sources, the White House contacted Comey and invited him to have a beer with the president on the White House lawn.

"When Jim's appointments secretary read him the message, he was taken by complete surprise," a source familiar with the exchange between the White House and Comey said in an interview for this book. "The request wasn't proper, and Jim told his secretary to tell the White House he was too busy to have a casual beer with the president.

"Jim didn't think more about it for a few weeks, until the president himself called," the source continued. "Obama made small talk and said he'd like to have a one-on-one basketball game with Jim. He said he'd heard that Jim had a hoop at home.

"Jim is a lifelong cop and prosecutor and his mind always goes to motive. What did the president really want to talk about? Jim was certain that Obama wanted to pressure him regarding the Hillary investigation.

"Jim told Obama that he'd love to have a one-on-one with him, but he begged off saying his schedule was a killer and he couldn't justify taking the time away from his job. Jim told me that Obama sounded really pissed off. Jim was surprised that Obama, Mr. Cool himself, had stepped over the line."

By late fall—on the eve of Election Day—Obama was beyond pissed off; he was fed up with Comey and was considering removing him from his job. In a series of conversations that have never been reported before, Obama and Jarrett discussed the political and legal ramifications of firing the FBI head. According to highly reliable sources with knowledge of these conversations, the president was reluctant to move against Comey for fear that doing so would open him to charges of obstruction of justice.

However, according to the sources, Jarrett convinced the president that there would be bipartisan support in Congress for a move against Comey. The White House counsel agreed with Jarrett, and Obama ordered his top advisers to draw up a plan for ridding himself of the troublesome FBI director.

"But as in so many other cases during his presidency, Obama's Hamlet side took over," said the source. "He dithered and dithered and never pulled the trigger."

■   ■   ■

"The extent of the Obama White House's interference continued to be a sore point with Jim even after Obama left office," the FBI source said. "Jim knew that [Attorney General Loretta] Lynch had planted several Obama loyalists from the Justice Department in the FBI, and that they remained there into the new Trump administration.

"He had solid intelligence that a number of people in the FBI were Obama moles who were playing a double game, and he was determined to get to the bottom of the problem," the source went on. "Late one night in February, he summoned the heads of the bureau's departments and their deputies to his office for a showdown. He told me all about it later.

"He questioned them individually, one by one. He wanted to root out anyone who was the least bit disloyal. Each of the interviews lasted about twenty minutes. He demanded names, dates, and specific incidents, and he took notes in long hand.

"He told me that he was in a nasty mood that night. He paced the floor and got so angry that at one point he snapped a pencil in half with his fingers. He's an aggressive prosecutor who knows all the tricks of the trade, including how to use his height [Comey is six-foot-eight] to intimidate people. He towered over some of the men and women he questioned, often pointing his finger in their faces.

"He told me that he used what he called 'the basketball steal.' I've seen him do it. For a big man, he's amazingly quick on his feet, and during the interrogations, he'd suddenly spring out of his chair and move so fast around the desk that it appeared he was going to pounce.

"Sometimes, he raised his voice, practically yelling, and he told me that a few of the bureau chiefs and their deputies left his office looking like they'd been taken to the woodshed.

"He explained to me that he purposely chose to meet with the staff late at night, because he wanted them to be uncomfortable and off guard.

"After a couple of hours of questioning, he told an assistant that he was hungry and wanted something to eat, and he sent him to the Capitol Grill [a favorite FBI and Justice Department hangout located on Pennsylvania Avenue] to get him a Caesar salad, a bone-in ribeye steak, and mashed potatoes. Plus, a cheesecake for desert.

"An FBI porter set his office table with a white tablecloth and decanted a bottle of a California Zinfandel. Jim dined listening to

Brahms. When he got to the cheesecake, he asked his senior lieutenants to come to his office. He offered each of them a glass of wine. Most turned down the wine.

"Jim told them that he had uncovered a number of people he suspected of being disloyal. He named several of them. At one point, he pounded his desk for emphasis and said that there was going to be a major overhaul of the team. But before he had a chance to do the house-cleaning, Trump fired him."

32

THE COMEY AFFAIR: PART II

C omey had worn out his welcome in Washington long before he got on the wrong side of Trump.

Republicans didn't trust him because, as assistant attorney general in 2004, he had threatened to resign over former President George W. Bush's post-9/11 domestic intelligence program. Democrats despised him for damaging Hillary's chances of becoming president. As a result, Trump expected a round of applause from both sides of the aisle for getting rid of the FBI director. Instead, the Democrats and their lapdogs in the media compared the firing to Watergate and Nixon's Saturday Night Massacre.

The comparison was absurd. Trump had more than sufficient justification to get rid of Comey. Any lingering doubts about that were dispelled by Deputy Attorney General Rod Rosenstein, who drew up a devastating bill of particulars.

"I cannot defend the Director's handling of the conclusion of the investigation of secretary Clinton's e-mails," Rosenstein wrote in a memo to Trump. "And I do not understand his refusal to accept the nearly universal judgment that he was mistaken. Almost everyone agrees that the Director made serious mistakes; it is one of the few issues that unites people of diverse perspectives.

"The Director was wrong to usurp the Attorney General's authority on July 5, 2016, and announce his conclusion that the case should be closed without prosecution," Rosenstein continued. "It is not the function of the Director to make such an announcement. At most, the Director should have said the FBI had completed its investigation and presented the findings to the federal prosecutors.

"In response to skeptical questions at a congressional hearing, the Director defended his remarks by saying that his 'goal was to say what is true. What did we do, what did we find, what do we think about it.' But the goal of a federal criminal investigation is not to announce our thoughts at a press conference. The goal is to determine whether there is sufficient evidence to justify a federal criminal prosecution, then allow a federal prosecutor who exercises authority delegated by the Attorney General to make a prosecutorial decision, and then—if prosecution is warranted—to let the judge and jury determine the facts."

■ ■ ■

Before he drew up the final version of his memo, Rosenstein asked Andrew McCabe, the deputy director of the FBI, to come to his office at the Justice Department. He told McCabe that he was thinking of recommending to the president that Comey be replaced, but that before he went ahead with such a major decision, he wanted McCabe's candid opinion of Comey's handling of his job.

McCabe was known among his colleagues at the FBI as both highly intelligent and highly ambitious. He could also, they said, be slippery. When his wife, Dr. Jill McCabe, ran an unsuccessful campaign for a seat in the Virginia state senate, she received a $700,000 contribution from a political action committee controlled by Virginia Governor Terry

McAuliffe, a close Clinton ally. McCabe, who was deeply involved in the Hillary email investigation, failed to disclose his conflict of interest. Asked why he left out that information on his financial disclosure forms, a McCabe spokesman said, "The form does not require that an employee spouse's salary be disclosed." Of course, the $700,000 wasn't a salary; it was a political contribution from a major Hillary confidant.

"While many F.B.I. agents try to chart career paths out in the field by making cases and arrests—and avoiding the politics of Washington—Mr. McCabe has stayed here [in Washington] and thrived," reported the *New York Times*' Adam Goldman and Matt Apuzzo. "He sometimes comes off at the F.B.I. as rigid, particularly in comparison with the more outgoing Mr. Comey. But Mr. McCabe, a triathlete known for biking 35 miles to work from Virginia, has stood out for his intellect and the range of high-profile cases he has been at the center of."

McCabe would later testify before a Senate committee that he held Comey "in the absolute highest regard." But that was not what he told Rosenstein during their secret meeting, which has not been reported until now.

McCabe had long wanted Comey's job. He believed that he had earned it, and he was willing to stab his boss in the back to get it. He told Rosenstein that Comey deserved to be fired.

When Comey learned about the Rosenstein-McCabe meeting from a close friend at the Justice Department, he was devastated.

"Jim thought Andy was loyal, and he trusted him implicitly," said a source who discussed the matter with Comey. "He was shocked to learn that McCabe met with Rosenstein in secret and never told him about it.

"I wouldn't say that Andy and Jim were great friends, but they were certainly very collegial, worked together all the time, and put in very late hours together," the source continued. "They would have a drink after work occasionally, go to the Capitol Grill for dinner. They'd put a hand on each other's shoulder when they talked, that sort of thing.

"In his meeting with Rosenstein, McCabe attacked Jim's decision-making, particularly with regard to the Hillary Clinton investigation. He told Rosenstein that Jim's judgment was seriously flawed when he made the decision not to prosecute Hillary—a decision that should have been left to the prosecutors at Justice. McCabe also said Comey had politicized the Clinton email case beyond resurrection, and that he had been out of bounds when he went on television and gave a news conference about a suspect [Hillary] whom he was simultaneously clearing of criminal activity.

"McCabe also told Rosenstein that Jim's personal conduct was inconsistent with acceptable behavior for a director of the FBI. He cited as an example Jim's late-night marathon interrogation of his staff, and his lavish steak dinner while he dined alone and listened to Brahms.

"Naturally, Jim felt betrayed. He knew that he'd put some noses out of joint in the bureau as a result of his gruff handling of the senior staff. But he thought he was doing it for the good of the bureau, and he expected that the people he roughed up would understand that it wasn't personal.

"Up to a point, Jim was right about that. It wasn't personal for McCabe. It was his ambition for power."

■ ■ ■

With Rosenstein's indictment of Comey in hand, Trump could have summoned Comey to the White House, asked for his resignation, and issued a press release acknowledging Comey's years of public service. That would have been the conventional move. Instead, Trump fired the director without notice and while he was away from Washington.

It was a public humiliation. But Trump went further than that. He told NBC News' Lester Holt that he'd been planning to fire Comey even before he received Rosenstein's recommendation, and that he was motivated, at least in part, by Comey's Russian investigation.

"In fact, when I decided to just do it," Trump told Holt, "I said to myself, I said, 'You know, this Russia thing with Trump and Russia is a made-up story. It's an excuse by the Democrats for having lost an election that they should have won.'"

The villains jumped on Trump's statement as evidence he had obstructed justice.

But that was absurd.

"When a deputy attorney general concluded that Director Comey usurped the role of the Department of Justice in his decision not to recommend prosecution of Hillary Clinton, President Trump made the only legally correct call, to fire the director," said Elizabeth Price Foley, a professor of law at Florida International University. "The country deserves an FBI director who respects his limited role as an investigator, and whose reputation is not sullied by inappropriately political behavior."

■ ■ ■

"Jim had no inkling he was about to be fired," a close friend said in an interview for this book. "He hadn't heard the gossip that he was on his way out. He learned about it while addressing his agents in the Los Angeles field office about new surveillance and encryption techniques.

"When the report flashed on the TV, he thought it was a joke," his friend continued. "But then he got a call from Andy McCabe, who told him that Keith Schiller [Trump's longtime bodyguard] had delivered a letter to FBI headquarters dismissing Comey and appointing him [McCabe] acting director.

"Jim was in a state of shock. Arrangements were made to get him to LAX, and when word got out that his caravan of cars was headed to the airport, TV news helicopters followed him as he was on his way.

"He boarded the Justice Department's Gulfstream, and started barking orders at his assistants both on the plane and on the telephone back in Washington. He called the White House and asked to be put through to the president. No one at the White House would take his calls.

"He put in a call to his wife, Patrice, who was in tears. She told him that the way his dismissal was handled made it look as though he had committed some horrible misdeed. He told Patrice to pray for him, then he closed his eyes and prayed as his plane made its way home."

■ ■ ■

Trump's tweet suggesting he might have tape recordings of his conversation with Comey turned out to be a bluff. And the bluff boomeranged.

Testifying before the Senate intelligence committee, Comey said that Trump's tape trick caused him to leak the memo of the conversation he had with Trump about swearing his loyalty. But instead of leaking the memo himself, he gave it to a friend—a professor at Columbia University—who sent it to a reporter at the *New York Times*. His goal, Comey said, was to trigger the appointment of a special counsel to investigate the president.

Comey's scheme—and "scheme" was the only word for it—worked. Newspapers, TV networks, and the Internet ran with Comey's version of the story—namely, that Trump had asked him to swear loyalty and to drop his investigation of Michael Flynn. As a result of the controversy, Rod Rosenstein appointed Robert Mueller as a special counsel to lead the Russian probe.[1]

"Far from keeping Mr. Comey quiet," editorialized the *Wall Street Journal*, "Mr. Trump's 'tapes' tweet led to the creation of a mortal threat to his presidency."

■ ■ ■

"By his actions, Comey [who for most of his career was a registered Republican] reveals himself to be a fellow traveler with Never Trumpers," wrote Michael Goodwin. "His firing brought him out of the shadows and into the open 'resistance' to the president. Curiously for a man who claims to be nonpartisan, Comey wasn't bothered nearly as much when a Democratic attorney general tried to meddle in the election by smothering his investigation of Hillary Clinton's emails. Or when the IRS went after conservatives."

"If Comey didn't trust a duly elected president," Goodwin continued, "the honorable thing would be to resign. But Comey was not honorable. Instead, he was a sneaky note-taker collecting grievances as insurance for himself. But he didn't create a national crisis alone. He colluded with the anti-Trump media, which recognized the FBI director as a kindred spirit; he cemented their brotherhood with leaks."

The takeaway: the timing and manner of Comey's firing could have been handled with more finesse. But faced with an FBI director whose heart was with the villains in the "resistance," Trump did the right thing and got rid of a treacherous agent within his ranks.

33

THE VULGARIANS

T he villains complained all the time about Donald Trump's "vulgar" attacks on his enemies. How could a president stoop so low! He degraded the office of the presidency! And so on. But the fact was, Trump's attacks paled by comparison with the savage assaults that were launched against him.

From the beginning of his presidency, Trump was under a relentless verbal siege. The attacks were unprecedented in their gush of fury and vitriol. No modern president had been treated with less respect than he was. The villains discarded all the traditional rules regarding political discourse. In doing so, they—not Trump—became the embodiment of the vulgarity they decried.

There were endless examples of this coarse and often obscene behavior. But here are six that I've chosen as the most outrageous:

1. After Trump called CBS' *Face the Nation* fake news, the network's late-night host Stephen Colbert came to the defense of the Sunday news show's host, John Dickerson. Colbert went on an obscene rant against the president. "Mr. President," Colbert said, "I love your presidency. I call it Disgrace the Nation. You're not POTUS, you're the gloat-us. You're the glutton with the button. You're a regular Gorge Washington. You're the presi-dunce but you're turning into a real prick-tator. You attract more skinheads than free Rogaine. You have more people marching against you than cancer. You talk like a sign-language gorilla that got hit in the head. In fact, the only thing your mouth is good for is being Vladimir Putin's cock holster." It was the most shocking verbal assault on a president in living memory, and many commentators pointed out that if Colbert had employed the same kind of "humor" against Barack Obama, he would have been fired on the spot. He wasn't. Colbert's only apology was directed at gays and lesbians; he was sorry, he said, if they interpreted his remark about "cock holster" as homophobic.

2. Jimmy Kimmel targeted Trump when he hosted the Oscars. He had the Hollywood celebrities in stitches with this one-liner: "Some of you will get to come up on this stage tonight and give a speech that the president of the United States will tweet about in all caps during his 5 a.m. bowel movement tomorrow." There was not a word of disapproval from Kimmel's bosses at ABC about his use of toilet humor on primetime TV before an audience that included young children. Nor did the Federal Communications Commission, which has an obscenity rule that prohibits the broadcast of content that depicts sexual or excretory activity, take any action against ABC.

3. When Oskar Eustis, the longtime artistic director of the Public Theater in New York City, decided to stage a

modern version of Shakespeare's *Julius Caesar*, he presented Caesar as Donald Trump, complete with a mop of yellow hair and an extra-long red tie. Caesar's wife, Calpurnia, appeared as Melania Trump, a statuesque model with a Slovenian accent. The Roman mob was meant to resemble a frenzied Trump rally. New York audiences roared with delight when Caesar/Trump was slain and lay in a pool of his own blood. The message from the Public Theater was clear: it was okay to depict the assassination of the president of the United States.

4. CNN's morning show *New Day* regularly denounced Trump for his "misogyny," but a secret recording by James O'Keefe's Project Veritas caught Jimmy Carr, one of the show's producers, trashing White House counselor Kellyanne Conway for her appearance. "She looks like she got hit with a shovel," said Carr. He also admitted in the stealth recording that CNN's boss, Jeff Zucker, encouraged his staff to focus on the Trump-Russia story in order to attract higher ratings. Zucker's strategy worked: as a result of CNN's relentless anti-Trump coverage, the network saw double-digit ratings growth.

5. The villains jumped on Trump when he posted a tweet about *Morning Joe*'s co-host Mika Brzezinski. Oh, how could he say such a thing about a woman! How could he talk about her facelift! The *Washington Times*' Charles Hurt took the "puritanical schoolmarms of the political press" to task for going "bonkers" over Trump's tweet. Said Hurt: "They scolded him that his Twitter missives were beneath the office of the president. Really, you mean like molesting an intern in the Oval Office? 'Presidential' like that?"

6. In the aftermath of a terrorist attack on London Bridge, Trump tweeted, "We need to be smart, vigilant and tough. We need the courts to give us back our rights. We need the

Travel Ban as an extra level of safety!" That didn't sit well
with Reza Aslan, the host of CNN's weekly show *Believer.*
"This piece of shit is not just an embarrassment to America and a stain on the presidency," said Aslan. "He's an
embarrassment to humankind." The embarrassment was
Aslan, who was dropped by the network, but who remains
a hero to the Left.

34

CAMPUS MAYHEM

"The FBI is concerned with violence and potential violence, not with stupid comments by talk show hosts like Stephen Colbert," a former Justice Department official, who now works as a consultant with the FBI, said in an interview for this book. "Celebrities who incite violence against the president, like Kathy Griffin, are the province of the Secret Service.

"Since Trump's election, the bureau has been concentrating on 'resistance' groups that have either committed acts of violence or are planning to carry out violent actions," the FBI consultant continued. "The bureau has discovered that these groups are carrying out training all across the country. They are teaching recruits how to make improvised deadly weapons such as baseball bats with spikes, heavy metal clubs, and loose ball bearings that can be tossed in the street to disable law enforcement officers. The training sessions have taken place in college gyms and in the basements of churches, where there is sympathy for the radical movement.

"There's evidence that these groups are moving up to more sophisticated devices, like improvised bombs. The majority of violent activists aren't students, but the agitators focus their activities in college towns, because they provide them with cover and recruitment. There are chapters of violent groups at college towns all across the country—Madison, New York, Newark, Boston, and Berkeley."

■　■　■

The University of California, Berkeley, was the scene of the most violent protests. Masked agitators dressed in black, many of whom belonged to an anarchist group called Antifa (short for anti-fascist), shattered windows, smashed doors, set cars afire, threw smoke bombs, firebombs, and urine-filled bottles at the police, set off fireworks, and attacked pro-Trump demonstrators with baseball bats, rocks, bricks, and knives. The authorities at the university locked down the campus and canceled a speech by the conservative provocateur Milo Yiannopoulos, and forced author Ann Coulter to call off her scheduled appearance.

"The Left is absolutely terrified of free speech and will do literally anything to shut it down," Yiannopoulos said on Facebook about the events at Berkeley. He hardly needed to underscore the irony that Berkeley had once been the home of the so-called "free-speech movement."

"Multiple methods of crowd control were in place," the university said in a press release that tried to defend its ineffectual response to the violence. "Ultimately and unfortunately, however it was simply impossible to maintain order given the level of threat, disruption and violence."[1]

The Berkeley city government, which is among the most leftwing in America, was either unable or unwilling to mount a strong response to the riots. Mayor Jesse Arreguin, thirty-one, was himself a member of BAMN, the acronym for By Any Means Necessary, one of the violent groups that participated in the protests. When the FBI's San Francisco field office sent a team of agents to Berkeley, they received a tepid welcome from university officials and the police.

The FBI's investigation of the violence at Berkeley was the subject of a field report, delivered to Acting Director Andrew McCabe on July 11.

The report, which is being published for the first time in this book, painted an alarming picture of a nationwide network of radical groups that was bent on sowing confusion and chaos, and overthrowing the Trump presidency.[2]

"This is the greatest challenge to law enforcement since the Weather Underground and the Black Panther Party," the report declared.[3]

The FBI found that members of the anarchist groups were able to hide on many campuses, because they could "count on the fact that they will get protection from the academic community." College administrators and professors might not agree with the extreme violence practiced by the radicals, the report pointed out, "but they clearly agree with them on resistance to the current [Trump] administration's perceived policies and goals."

The report continued: "The universities across the country, where the radicals operate, are extremely useful for their goals. They use the school's facilities to make posters to be distributed to resistance protesters. The college drama departments have been used in many cases to make masks and other disguises.

"Electronic bulletin boards are used to quickly get word out to like-minded students about the dates and places of marches. These bulletin boards are often closed groups, meaning that only students can access them.

"When they are injured in violent confrontations with police, they can seek treatment at student health facilities with reasonable assurance the incident will not be reported to police the way a public or private hospital or clinic would likely do in the wake of violent street clashes."

■ ■ ■

The FBI report compared the organization of the violent "resistance" movement on American college campuses to the loose structure of radical Islamist groups.

"Members are only united by a common ideology and a love of inflicting violence upon those perceived as the enemy," the report said. "They all agree that chaos and violence against the government and business institutions—particularly banking—is a positive good.

"It's not the kind of thing that needs to be written down or even much discussed. There are no membership rolls, no rules, and no hierarchy of leadership. The goal is simple and unstated: violent assaults with no warning or apparent reason. That is the nature of terror and the reason it is so terrifying.

"Often splinter groups on college campuses are formed into groups with innocuous names and benign purposes, like 'The Bird Watchers,' but most hide under pro-environmental names."

According to the FBI report, these harmless-sounding groups received funding from universities, and used the universities' facilities to meet and hide their equipment.

"We have information," the authors of the report wrote, "that there are numerous caches of weaponized tools and the ingredients to manufacture improvised explosive devices on college campuses across the country.

"Universities have a rather unique status as sanctuaries for undocumented aliens and even criminal anarchists. The hardest thing to predict is: When will the next assault occur?"

35

THE ISIS CONNECTION

The FBI's investigation of the radical "resistance" movement on college campuses led to a major discovery—the collusion between the American anarchists and foreign terrorists.

"There is clearly overwhelming evidence that there are growing ties between U.S. radicals and the Islamic State, as well as several [ISIS] offshoots and splinter group affiliates," the FBI report concluded.

The FBI had been keeping tabs on efforts by the Islamic State to recruit followers among violent anarchist groups in the United States. In early July, the bureau dispatched a task force to report on the massive demonstrations planned by radical groups, such as the German contingent Antifaschistische Aktion, to protest President Trump's first trip to Europe. Trump flew to Poland, where he delivered a stirring speech in defense of the values of Western civilization. He then traveled to Hamburg, Germany, for a meeting of the leaders and central bank governors of the G20 group of major industrialized countries.

In the weeks leading up to the G20 summit, European leftists opposed to free market capitalism set fires on German railway lines. On the eve of the summit, masked rioters and other militants joined a "Welcome to Hell March," which swelled to nearly 80,000 protesters. The German government deployed riot police, who demanded that the marchers remove their masks. When they refused, the police responded with batons and water cannon.

Among the ranks of masked marchers were anarchists from the United States profiled in the FBI's subsequent report.

■ ■ ■

"Task force covered G-20 meeting in Hamburg, studied intel from local authorities, Interpol, and other assets, determined that as assumed U.S.-based anarchist/radical groups had traveled to Germany and took place in the violence," the FBI's summary stated. "There is also evidence of meetings between these individuals and associates of ISIS. There is an urgent need to closely surveil the identified individuals."

The agents sent by the FBI paid particular attention to a group of anarchists from Oakland, a major port city that lies adjacent to Berkeley in the San Francisco Bay Area.

"Ties between three key leaders of the Oakland group [names redacted] met in Hamburg with a leader of the AQAP [Al Qaeda in the Arabian Peninsula] and the AQIM [Al Qaeda in the Islamic Maghreb]," the report said. "The leader from AQAP is an Egyptian born male [name redacted] who is known to be in charge of finances and recruiting for the group.

"There is evidence from informants that he is helping the Oakland group acquire the weapons they are seeking, primarily bomb making equipment and toxic chemicals and gasses.

"One of the men from Oakland traveled to Syria to meet with ISIS, the purpose was for training in tactics, but was thought to be primarily a bonding visit to discuss possible massive disruptive attacks on the U.S.

"While in Hamburg several of the Oakland-based criminals were photographed throwing Molotov cocktails and wielding iron bars, which have been their weapons of choice, though they are almost certainly on the verge of upping the caliber of their weaponry for use in the U.S.

"Despite having their faces covered by masks they were positively identified.

"This group and their connections with the radical Islamic groups must be disrupted and destroyed.

"Action has been taken with the appropriate agencies to see that these named individuals will be identified when they return to the United States. It has not been determined if they will be detained or surveilled...

"Numerous interviews have been carried out by associates of this group and have yielded some actionable intelligence, but the decision is to wait until the movement can be infiltrated and it is guaranteed that all criminal behavior can be identified and successfully prosecuted before any move is made."

36

A RED FLAG

During his investigation of Hillary's emails, former FBI Director James Comey set up a hotline with Mireille Ballestrazzi, the head of INTERPOL, the International Criminal Police Organization. Thanks to Ballestrazzi and INTERPOL's worldwide resources, Comey collected intelligence on the interconnections between Middle Eastern jihadis, European radicals, and the American anarchists who were part of the anti-Trump "resistance" movement.

"The Americans communicate with the Islamic State and other terrorist organizations on websites, and they use those websites to download instructions for making weapons," said an FBI source who had access to Comey's intelligence, which supplemented and expanded on the written "Informational Reports" described in the previous two chapters of this book. "As the Trump administration has demonstrated it's serious about destroying the Islamic State, and depriving ISIS of territory in Iraq and Syria, the alliance between the American radicals and ISIS has grown even closer. The Internet chatter between the Americans and the Islamists is astronomical.

"The FBI is really playing catchup ball, because the Obama administration refused to give the Bureau the resources it needed to effectively infiltrate and surveil the radical groups on college campuses," the source continued. "Any talk of a connection between radical Islam—a phrase the Obama people wouldn't even use—and American extremists was pretty much laughed off. Loretta Lynch would have blown a gasket if she heard that the FBI was surveilling so-called college political organizations.

"All that's changed under the Trump administration. Everyone's aware that the resistance movement, with its effort to get rid of Trump by any means necessary, has created fertile soil for ISIS and al Qaeda to establish a beachhead in America. And the FBI now has the manpower to keep track of the radicals and surveil them if they travel to Syria and meet face to face with jihadis.

"Our biggest concern, of course, is that the anarchists will get the training they need to make weapons of mass destruction. That's something that acts like a red flag. We can't allow that to happen."

37

"MALIGNANT MASTERPIECES OF VICTIMHOOD"

When Hillary Clinton declared on St. Patrick's Day that she was ready to "come out of the woods" and lead the "resistance" to Donald Trump, you could almost hear groans of anguish coming from certain quarters of the Democratic Party.

The Democrats were sick and tired of losing elections (they'd lost 1,042 state and federal posts under Obama), but many of them seriously doubted that Hillary was the answer to their problems. Some joked that she was like Monty Woolley in the classic movie *The Man Who Came to Dinner*; she wouldn't shut up and go away.

Not all Democrats felt that way, of course, but the politically astute understood that an in-your-face Hillary would be a godsend to Republicans—a twice-defeated presidential candidate who, according to the polls, had lost popularity among those who voted for her in 2016, and who was now more unpopular than Donald Trump.

"The more Clinton weighs in and tries to tell voters 'I'm baaack,' the more Republicans will tell her to keep on trucking," said Doug Heye, a Republican strategist.

Not surprisingly, Hillary didn't care what either the Democrats or Republicans thought. She was looking for redemption and another shot at the presidency.

"She hates Donald Trump to the point of obsession," a Hillary confidante said in an interview for this book. "She wants to be the leader of the opposition, and she's planning to raise money and travel around the country, making speeches for Democrats in the midterms and collecting chits for 2020.

"She's absolutely convinced voters will realize what a horrible mistake they made in electing Trump, and beg her to run again," the close friend continued. "Many of her former campaign people, like Brian Fallon [her press secretary] and Zac Petkanas [the chief of her rapid-response team], feed her ambitions for their own selfish reasons; they're eager to make up for the way they bungled the 2016 election, and find employment in a future Hillary campaign.

"Bill's warned Hillary about engaging in impeachment talk against Trump. When Bill was impeached, he actually became more popular. The same could happen to Trump.

"She turned to Obama for help, and met with him in Kalorama, but she came away completely disillusioned. She said Obama laughs the whole Trump thing off. He's got no stomach for it. He doesn't give a fig about her future. It's just as well that Obama's not out front in the resistance movement, because with the dark mood Hillary's in, they'd be fighting nonstop. Right now, her anger is eating her up."

■ ■ ■

Was Hillary Clinton a major player in the plot to destroy Trump? Or was she a washed-up politician? Many of the people I interviewed for this book wondered whether she was in shape, physically or psychologically, to lead the "resistance."

She had been gaining weight, letting her hair and makeup go, paying less attention to her wardrobe, drinking heavily, and saying weird things such as that Bernie Sanders' attacks during the primaries had caused her "lasting damage." The *New York Post's* Maureen Callahan said that Hillary was so delusional about her chances for a comeback that she'd become "the Norma Desmond of American politics, still waiting for her close-up."

It was a political platitude that Hillary blamed everyone but herself for her election loss—especially Russian hackers and James Comey. But in a series of rambling and sometimes incoherent interviews, she invented a whole new list of culprits whom she held responsible for her defeat.

Her top five list:

Culprit No. 1. During a conversation with Christiane Amanpour at a Women for Women luncheon in New York City, Hillary blamed members of the news media for failing to press Trump hard enough on policy details during the presidential debates. Their failure was a major reason for her loss, she insisted.

It was a ludicrous charge, since most reporters had been in her pocket during the campaign, and had been plenty tough on Trump.

"Hillary attacking the media is totally misguided," tweeted CNN's Chris Cillizza, who had been one of her most vocal cheerleaders. "We asked Trump for specifics on his plans over and over again."

Culprit No. 2. During a question and answer session at the annual Code Conference in Rancho Palos Verdes, California, Hillary blasted the Democratic National Committee for its lack of support during the campaign.

"So I'm now the nominee of the Democratic Party," she recalled. "I inherit nothing from the Democratic Party. I mean, it was bankrupt. It was on the verge of insolvency. Its data was mediocre to poor, nonexistent, wrong. I had to inject money into it."[1]

It was a bizarre accusation, since the chairwoman of the DNC, Debbie Wasserman Schulz, had done everything in her power to help Hillary win the nomination, including limiting the number of primary debates to six, defending the system of superdelegates, and shutting down Bernie

Sanders' access to the DNC's voter data base. Wasserman Schulz's pro-Hillary bias was so fanatical that she was forced to resign.

Culprit No. 3. Hillary argued that Russian hackers were mysteriously "guided by Americans" and other political operatives.

"The overriding issue that affected the election that I had any control over—because I had no control over the Russians—was the way the use of my email account was turned into the greatest scandal since Lord knows when," she said. "This was the biggest nothing burger ever.

"The Russians, in my opinion, and based on the intel and counter-intel people I've talked to, could not have known how best to weaponize that information unless they had been guided," she continued. "Guided by Americans and guided by people who had polling and data information.

"I think it's fair to ask, how did that actually influence the campaign, and how did they know what messages to deliver? Who told them? Who were they coordinating with, and colluding with?"

Asked by one of the moderators whether she was "leaning Trump," Hillary replied: "Yes, I'm leaning Trump. I think it's pretty hard not to."

Culprit No. 4. Hillary lashed out at those who criticized her paid speeches to Goldman Sachs. Men had been paid for such speeches, she complained, and nobody criticized *them*. They were holding her to a different standard, because she was a woman.

"At some point, it bleeds into misogyny," she said. "And let's just be honest, you know, people who have...a set of expectations about who should be president and what a president looks like, you know, they're going to be much more skeptical and critical of somebody who doesn't look like and talk like and sound like everybody else who's been president. Anyway, you know, President Obama broke that racial barrier, but you know, he's a very attractive, good-looking *man*."

Culprit No. 5. "Bill didn't do enough to help me win," Hillary groused to her friends. "First, his health didn't allow him to make enough appearances. Second, he disagreed with my campaign strategy and was in a snit about it most of the time. And third, he didn't have his heart in the campaign, because he really didn't relish the prospect of returning to the White House and giving up the life of playboy of the Western world."

All of this was too much for Peggy Noonan, the Pulitzer Prize-winning columnist of the *Wall Street Journal*, who had been kind to Hillary in defeat and hard on Trump in victory.

"Her public statements since defeat have been malignant little masterpieces of victimhood—claiming, blame-shifting and unhelpful accusations," Noonan wrote. "They deserve censure."

■ ■ ■

To take the measure of Hillary's state of mind—and judge her fitness for the role of chief villain in the anti-Trump resistance—I turned to a woman who has known Hillary since her days at Wellesley College, and who has spent a great deal of time with her since her election loss. The friend recalled a day in late May that she and a group of women spent with Hillary at her home in Chappaqua. The conversation was reconstructed from memory.

"We sat around the pool under umbrellas," the friend began. "Several bottles of California Chardonnay were chilling on a nearby table. At first, the talk was mostly about grandchildren and old college friends, who, like us, are getting up in years. But after an hour of dangling our legs in the pool, someone asked Hillary, 'What's next for you?'

"'I guess I'm retired,' Hillary said.

"She gave a short, mirthless laugh.

"She stood and said, 'Let's go inside and have a real drink.'

"In the family room, Hillary sat on a couch with pillows. When she realized the pillow she was hugging had the seal of the President of the United States on it, she tossed it across the room.

"A housekeeper wheeled in a silver bar cart with alcohol, mixers, and ice. Hillary got up and made us a round of gin and tonics.

"One of the women said, 'We've known you forever. You don't have it in you to give up. We know you have a big plans. Spill the beans.'

"'Well, you're right,' Hillary said. 'I'm never giving up. But truthfully, I'm not operating on all eight cylinders yet. My mind wanders, and I find it hard to concentrate. I don't feel like making a big decision right now.'

"She continued: 'Bill says I've been drinking too much, and I probably am, but for the first time in years, I don't have to make urgent strategic decisions. So Bill can fuck off. He can put up with my stumbling and feeling sorry for myself for a while.'

"One of the women made a second round of gin and tonics. We were getting a little high.

"Hillary said that Huma [Abedin] had really helped her get through the roughest patches after her loss. She said. 'I couldn't have made it without her. I don't think I would have gotten out of bed some days.'

"She said, 'I know I sound as though I'm always blaming other people, but I can't help it. They screwed me over. There was incompetence in the campaign, and I got bad advice. Plus, Bill's health didn't allow him to campaign as hard as he used to.'

"She said she was thinking about writing about her relationship with Barack Obama.

'There's a perception that Barack helped me politically,' she said. 'Made me secretary of state, then campaigned for me to succeed him. But the truth is, he needed me at State, because he didn't know what the hell he was doing. He had no knowledge of foreign affairs. None. He was learning as he went. I came to him with some big ideas about building coalitions in the Middle East and Asia. He liked them a lot, but then he went to Valerie and Michelle, and suddenly he didn't like my ideas anymore. Those two women controlled him completely. When Barack agreed on a plan of action, you knew it was likely he'd reverse himself the next day.'

"Hillary accepted a third drink, and started pacing the room. She couldn't get off the subject of the Obama years. She said the thing Obama bragged about the most—the killing of Osama Bin-Laden—almost didn't happen because Obama was always dithering.

"'He didn't want to okay the mission against Bin Laden,' she said. 'He was petrified the operation would turn into a disaster. In the days before the operation, he drafted a statement that he was going to issue if the Navy SEALs were killed or captured. He didn't have much faith in the SEAL team to pull it off. I know if I write about all that, I'll get no end of shit.'

"Hillary walked back to the couch and collapsed. She was completely out of steam, exhausted. She waved off another drink, and announced she was going to bed. She got up out of the couch, clearly with some difficulty, and headed out [of] the room, limping. Without turning around, she waved and said, 'Goddamn arthritis.'"

■ ■ ■

Three months later, Hillary's publisher, Simon & Schuster, teased out excerpts from her new book, *What Happened*. She lambasted Trump for his conduct during a presidential debate.

"It was the second presidential debate, and Donald Trump was looming behind me," she wrote. "Two days before, the world heard him brag about groping women. Now we were on a small stage and no matter where I walked, he followed me closely, staring at me, making faces.... It was one of those moments where you wish you could hit pause and ask everyone watching, 'Well, what would you do?' Do you stay calm, keep smiling and carry on as if he weren't repeatedly invading your space? Or do you turn, look him in the eye, and say loudly and clearly, 'Back up, you creep, get away from me!'"

Kellyanne Conway, a counselor to President Trump, had the best riposte to Hillary's fabricated description of what happened on the debate stage.

"This whole anecdote about a woman who is seeking the highest office in the land, if not the world, saying that a man was intimidating because of where he was standing at a debate," Conway said. "How are you going to stand up to the rest of the world's leaders if that was bothering you?"

Conway wasn't the severest critic of Hillary's book. That distinction fell to Bill Clinton.

"When Hillary gave Bill the manuscript of her book," said a close friend of the Clinton family, "he launched into a critique about how the book would be seen as a sniveling attempt to blame everybody but herself for her loss. He said she should have written about her hopes for the future of the country, not about her hurt feelings."

38

VILLAINS' REPORT CARD: THE DEMOCRATS

At their weekly closed-door caucus meeting on June 13, House Democrats got into a verbal brawl over the "i-word." Militants were obsessed with impeaching Trump. Shrewder heads questioned whether that was the best way to woo back lost voters.

"We believe strongly that a discussion about impeachment is not timely," Steny Hoyer, the minority whip, lectured the assembled congressmen.

Nancy Pelosi, the minority leader, cautioned patience.

"Trump will self-impeach," she said in a halfhearted attempt to appease her caucus.

The Democrat base was crying out for action against Trump, but Pelosi and Hoyer dreaded the prospect of having to vote on impeachment. They feared that such a vote, which had no chance of passing in the Republican-controlled House, would fire up the GOP base and make it harder for Democrats to win back control of the House in 2018.

That argument cut no ice with far-out liberals from California, the geographical heart of the "resistance."

"It's really the only way we can go," said Jackie Speier, who represented California's Fourteenth congressional district, which stretched from San Francisco to San Mateo County, two of the most liberal snake pits in the country.

Brad Sherman, an eleven-term congressman who represented Los Angeles' San Fernando Valley—where Democrats outnumbered Republicans five to one—said his patience had run out. He was ready to introduce an article of impeachment against the president, accusing Trump of obstructing justice when he fired FBI Director James Comey.

Pelosi and Hoyer rolled their eyes. The lunatics had taken over the asylum and threatened the future of the party.

■ ■ ■

A few weeks later, after Brad Sherman had introduced his impeachment bill, he appeared on Fox News' *Tucker Carlson Tonight*.

What did Sherman expect to achieve by such a pointless exercise? Carlson wanted to know.

Sherman hemmed and hawed, then finally admitted his bill was going nowhere—although he hoped it might trigger an "intervention" by White House aides, who could persuade Trump to abandon his reliance on Twitter.

Tucker Carlson's raucous laughter said it all: *lots of luck with that.*

The truth was, the more Democrats fixated on Trump, the less effective they were at the polls. In fact, their anti-Trump strategy was proving to be self-destructive. Since Trump's election, the Democrats had suffered three defeats in special elections to fill House seats.

"They are troubled most immediately by their failure to capture a seemingly winnable vacant House seat in suburban Atlanta," wrote the *Wall Street Journal's* Gerald F. Seib. "That has precipitated a round of backbiting and second-guessing, and a debate about whether the party's success lies in staking out the political center, to claim the votes of independents and moderate Republicans put off by the coarseness and unpredictability of Mr. Trump, or in moving left to capture and spread the passion of those who want a clean and sharp break from the status quo."

But the Democrats were caught on the horns of a dilemma. If they moved to the center in order to appeal to independents and moderates, they'd flout the wishes of their rich liberal donors who funded the "resistance" movement and whose chief political objective was getting rid of Donald Trump. Many of these donors pressed the leadership of the party to invoke the Twenty-Fifth Amendment, under which a majority of the Cabinet and the vice president could remove an unfit president from office.

Dennis Kucinich, the former Democratic congressman and presidential candidate, took his colleagues to task for pushing a bill that would establish an Oversight Commission on Presidential Capacity, whose sole aim was to examine Trump's mental qualifications to carry out his duties as president. The Trump-is-crazy-as-a-loon strategy, said Kucinich, "is destroying our party as an effective opposition."

■ ■ ■

Like Kucinich, many diehard Democrats started to reexamine their strategy. Maybe it wasn't Trump who was the problem; maybe it was the party's elitist attitude toward working class voters. Michael Tomasky, a Trump hater if there ever was one, wrote an article in the *New Republic* titled "Elitism is Liberalism's Biggest Problem." A piece in the far-left bi-monthly magazine *Mother Jones* was headlined "Less Liberal Contempt, Please."

"Much of what these authors write is sensible," noted William McGurn, a columnist for the *Wall Street Journal*. "But it can also be hilarious, particularly when the effort to explain ordinary Americans to progressive elites reads like a Margaret Mead entry on the exotic habits of the Samoans."

One sure sign of the Democrats' desperation was the groundswell of speculation about the presidential prospects of Kamala Harris, a former attorney general of California, who was the daughter of an Indian mother and a Jamaican-American father. A member of the U.S. Senate for less than a year, Harris was already being touted as "the next Barack Obama."[1] The *New York Times*, *Mother Jones*, and *The Hill* put the fifty-two-year-old Harris on their shortlist as a presidential candidate in 2020.

Harris scored points with the villains when she attacked Trump's attorney general, Jeff Sessions, at a Senate committee hearing. She badgered Sessions so ferociously that the committee's chairman had to warn her to allow the witness to answer her questions. The villains called the "shushing" of a woman by a male senator as an example of sexism—an absurd claim given the fact Harris violated the norms of the United States Senate. Nevertheless, her boorish behavior boosted Harris' stock among liberal Democrats.

"There's no question that a smart, experienced black woman vying for the White House could reanimate the Obama coalition in a way that Clinton wasn't able to," wrote Graham Vyse in the *New Republic*. "She'd be a new face nationally, without decades of political baggage, and an even bolder symbol of racial and gender progress than Obama or Clinton. Still, the hype about Harris is primarily a reflection of the weak Democratic bench."

It wasn't only their bench that was weak. The Democrats were devoid of ideas, and their problem began long before the arrival of Donald Trump on the political scene. It could be traced to the party's focus on cultural issues at the expense of pocketbook issues.

"Their focus on political correctness and conformity has left an impression on traditional Democrats that their party leaders care more about transgender bathroom access than employment, the cost of living, education or public safety," said Ted Van Dyk, a veteran Democratic operative. "Mrs. Clinton's 'deplorables' reference struck home with these voters.

"Millions of [voters], including traditional Democrats, driven by anger and frustration, abandoned their political roots last November to make Donald Trump president," Van Dyk continued. "Many probably sensed that chaos and fumbling would follow. By their lights, it was an acceptable price to pay to rid themselves of leaders who had forgotten them."

■ ■ ■

"When you lose to somebody who has 40 percent popularity, you don't blame other things—Comey, Russia—you blame yourself," said Chuck Schumer in a not-so-subtle dig at Hillary Clinton. "So what did we do wrong? People didn't know what we stood for, just that we were against Trump. And still believe that."

Proof of the Democrats' ideological bankruptcy came in late July when a clutch of Dems, including Nancy Pelosi, Elizabeth Warren, and Schumer (in shirtsleeves and sporting a large potbelly), showed up in a small town in Virginia and announced a new policy agenda for their party.

They named it "A Better Deal," and it contained a lot of recycled left-wing nostrums like a $15-an-hour minimum wage, paid family and sick leave, and lower prescription costs. Not surprisingly, it landed with a thud.

The Associated Press called it "a concoction that includes several parts Bernie Sanders, a few parts Obama, and a generous helping of Clinton." The wire service should have included "a blathering of Elizabeth Warren."

"What they thought they needed most in the midst of the Trumplosion was a slogan—and not even a good one," said Jonathan Allan, the co-author with Amie Parnes of *HRC*, an account of Hillary's time as secretary of state. "They should have kept their mouths shut and let voters think they were rudderless rather than announcing their mantra and removing all doubt.

"Here, in their infinite political savvy," Allan continued, "is what they've reportedly come up with: 'A Better Deal: Better Skills, Better Jobs, Better Wages.' The Twitterverse took about 10 seconds to compare the mantra to Papa John's 'Better Ingredients. Better Pizza.'"

■ ■ ■

In August, Barack Obama emerged from his room of solitude and sent out a tweet that became the most "liked" tweet of all time. Nearly three million people "liked" his tweet, in which he responded to the outbreak of racial violence in Charlottesville, Virginia, by quoting Nelson Mandela: "No one is born hating another person because of the color of his skin or his background or his religion…People must learn to hate, and if they can learn to hate, they can be taught love."

Strangely enough, Obama's sentiment virtually mirrored the reflections of Donald Trump. "When we open our hearts to patriotism," said the president, "there is no room for prejudice, no place for bigotry and no tolerance for hate." However, in Trump's case, it took four tries to get the substance and tone just right.

In his first response to Charlottesville, Trump blamed "many sides" for the day's tragic events, which left one woman dead and many people and policemen injured. He was censured for appearing to suggest that there was a moral equivalence between racists and anti-Semites and those resisting them.

In his second response, which he read from a Tel-a-Prompter, he denounced the KKK and Nazis by name—but he was nonetheless criticized for waiting two days to do so.

In his third response, which came during a combative press conference, he doubled down on his initial judgment that the march included "fine people" upset at Charlottesville's decision to pull down a statue of Robert E. Lee. What's more, he said that the "alt-left" counter-protesters, who included anarchists and Communists, should be held accountable for much of the violence. "You had the group on the other side that came charging in without a permit and they were very, very violent," he said.

Trump offered the media red meat with his comments on Charlottesville.

"The allegation that the mainstream media disseminates 'fake news' about the Trump administration often can seem overwrought, even a kind of caricature," writes Scott McConnell, a founding editor of *The American Conservative*. "Yet the nearly universal media response to President Trump's news conference at which he addressed the Charlottesville violence can only reinforce it. One day this response may make a rich subject for future historians analyzing it as earlier historians probed witch-burnings, pograms, and other outbreaks of mass hysteria.... Trump was making the same point as *New York Times* reporter Sheryl Gay Stolberg, who was on the ground in Charlottesville covering the event. She noticed that the far left counterprotesters were intent on instigating violence and tweeted that 'the hard left seemed as hate-filled as the alt-right. I saw club-wielding "antifa" beating white nationalists being led out of the park.'"

As I have reported in this book, extreme leftist groups like Antifa glorify violence, and Trump's remarks reflected a briefing by the FBI about Antifa's ferocious involvement in the Charlottesville mayhem. But his foundering response resulted in his biggest political crisis since the *Access Hollywood* tapes. CEOs on two White House advisory counsels quit en masse, a *New York Times* columnist ran a piece titled "Trump Makes Caligula Look Pretty Good," the Democrats jumped back on their impeachment bandwagon, and Trump's national economic director, Gary Cohn, who is Jewish, released a statement criticizing his boss.

The blowback emboldened angry leftists, who called for the removal of all "racist" symbols, which in their perfervid imagination included statues of Christopher Columbus, one of which was defaced in Baltimore.

"Once every Confederate monument in the country is down, what then?" asked Kyle Smith in *National Review*. "How is a statue of an ordinary rebel soldier in Durham, N.C., more offensive than a gorgeous building-sized tribute to slave-owning racist Thomas Jefferson on the Tidal Basin? We are reaching the point where, if the Washington Monument were to blow up tomorrow, it would be anyone's guess whether jihadists or the 'anti-fascist' Left did it."

39

VILLAINS' REPORT CARD: THE REPUBLICANS

For several months, Never-Trump Republicans had been unusually quiet. You didn't hear a lot of bellyaching from Bill Kristol at the *Weekly Standard* or snide comments from the editors at *National Review*. They seemed to have resigned themselves to the Trump presidency. But when Trump's firing of James Comey resulted in the appointment of a special counsel, and when Trump bobbled the ball on Charlottesville—when all that madness erupted in Washington, hell broke loose among Never-Trump Republicans.

John Kasich, the governor of Ohio, and one of the most unwavering Never-Trump Republicans, seized the opportunity to get back at Trump for the nasty things Trump had said about him during the primary campaign.

"I don't like people who say, 'I told you so,'" Kasich said. "But you know how much pressure, criticism, and heat I took because I was the one Republican who would not endorse Donald Trump, would not go to the convention. Some people thought I did it because I was angry or bitter. It had nothing to do with it. The things that have swirled around this White House are the reasons that caused me not to move forward and support him."

John McCain, who never missed an opportunity to take a dig at Trump, gloated over the Comey commotion, and severely criticized the president for his pardon of former Arizona sheriff Joe Arpaio. McCain tweeted: "@POTUS's pardon of Joe who illegally profiled Latinos, undermines his claim for the respect of law."

J. D. Hayworth, a former Republican congressman from Arizona and a host on Newsmax TV, had a few choice things to say about McCain.

"The dominant media culture, the leftist media, the partisan press, knows they can go nine times out of ten to McCain for a quote to trash Republicans," said Hayworth.

They could also count on McCain to look for an opportunity to get even with Trump for questioning his heroism. The opportunity arrived when McCain cast the crucial surprise nay that killed the Senate's Obamacare repeal vote, dooming Trump's chance to declare a major legislative victory.

And McCain didn't just cast a vote like every other senator. He waited until 1:29 a.m. before he reentered the Senate chamber. He waved to attract the attention of the Senate clerk, and then while everyone was watching, he gave a dramatic thumbs-down gesture indicating his "no" vote.

"McCain has 'a bit of a vindictive streak,'" Paul Begala wrote in *Third Term: Why George W. Bush (Hearts) John McCain.* "A former Pentagon official stated, 'John has an enemies list longer than Nixon's. And unlike Nixon, McCain really does try to get you.'"

Molly Hemingway, a senior editor at *The Federalist* and a Fox News contributor, had a different take on McCain and his fellow Never-Trump Republicans. At heart, she said, they were cold warriors who were appalled at Trump's effort to reach a rapprochement with Putin's Russia.

They were also appalled at Trump's manner and his refusal to be part of the Republican team that did things in the traditional Republican way. What's more, holier-than-thou Republicans like Senators Ben Sasse and Jeff Flake loved the adoration they received as Never-Trump Republicans from the liberal mainstream media.

But it also became apparent during the failure to repeal Obamacare, the opposition among some Republicans to Trump's proposed tax cuts, and his order that "transgender" individuals not be allowed to serve in the military, that Trump—for all the talk of his not being a "true conservative"—was more conservative than many of his conservative critics. Unlike them, he was determined to deliver on his campaign promises, and he had no interest in making a career in the swamp of Washington.

■ ■ ■

The best explanation of why so many Republicans were content to let the "resistance" treat Trump as a piñata came from Dennis Prager, the nationally syndicated talk-show host and columnist.

"I have concluded that there are a few reasons that explain conservatives who were NeverTrumpers during the election, and who remain anti-Trump today," Prager said. "The first and, by far, the greatest reason is this: They do not believe that America is engaged in a civil war, with the survival of America as we know it at stake. While they strongly differ with the Left, they do not regard the left-right battle as an existential battle for preserving our nation.

"To my amazement, no anti-Trump conservative writer sees it that way," he continued. "They all thought during the election, and still think, that while it would not have been a good thing if Hillary Clinton had won, it wouldn't have been a catastrophe.

"That's it, in a nutshell. Many conservatives, including me, believe that it would have been close to over for America as America if the Republican candidate, who happened to be a flawed man named Donald Trump, had not won."

Prager continued: "There is also a cultural divide. Anti-Trump conservatives are a very refined group of people. Trump doesn't talk like them. Moreover, the cultural milieu in which the vast majority of anti-Trump conservatives live and/or work means that to support Trump is to render oneself contemptible at all elite dinner parties.

"In addition, anti-Trump conservatives see themselves as highly moral people (which they often are) who are duty-bound not to compromise themselves by strongly supporting Trump, whom they largely view as morally defective.

"Finally, these people are only human. After investing so much energy in opposing Trump's election, and after predicting his nomination would lead to electoral disaster, it's hard for them to admit they were wrong."

■ ■ ■

When drawing up a report card on Republican villains, you had to give an F to Senator Susan Collins of Maine. During an appropriations subcommittee hearing, Collins was caught trashing Trump on a hot mike that someone had failed to switch off. The transcript of her private conversation with Jack Reed, a Democrat from Rhode Island, was leaked to the *Washington Post*.

"I swear, [the Trump administration's Office of Management and Budget] just went through and whenever there was 'grant,' they just X it out," Collins was heard telling Reed. "With no measurement, no thinking about it, no metrics, no nothing. It's just incredibly irresponsible."

"Yes, I think—I think he's crazy," Reed said in a reference to President Trump. "I mean, I don't say that lightly and as a kind of goofy guy."

"I'm worried," Collins agreed.

"Oof," Reed continued. "You know, this thing—if we don't get a budget deal, we're going to be paralyzed."

"I know," Collins replied.

"[The Department of Defense] is going to be paralyzed, everybody is going to be paralyzed," Reed said.

"I don't think [Trump] knows there is a [Budget Control Act] or anything," Collins said.

In another part of the transcript, Collins badmouthed Blake Farenthold, a Republican congressman from Texas, who had jokingly challenged her to a duel during a radio interview.

"Did you see the one who challenged me to a duel?" Collins asked Reed.

"I know," Reed replied. "Trust me. Do you know why he challenged you to a duel? 'Cause you could beat the shit out of him."

"Well, he's huge," Collins said. "And he—I don't mean to be unkind, but he's so unattractive it's unbelievable. Did you see the picture of him in his pajamas next to this Playboy bunny?"

At that point, the *Post* reported, the mike went dead.

■   ■   ■

Many Republicans were offended by President Trump's tweets humiliating and belittling Jeff Sessions. Trump reprimanded the attorney general for recusing himself from the Russian probe. As Trump saw it, Sessions' recusal opened the floodgates for the appointment of a special counsel to investigate whatever suited Robert Mueller's prosecutorial fancy.

Trump called it "a witch-hunt," which it appeared to be, since after more than a year of leaks and investigations, no one had yet come up with a shred of evidence to prove there had been collusion between Trump and the Russians.

"Exactly what crime is Trump suspected of committing?" asked Andrew McCarthy, a former assistant U.S. attorney for the Southern District of New York. "We all knew what Watergate was. We knew what Iran-Contra was. And the Lewinsky scandal. And the reported outing of Valerie Plame. Up until now, each time a special prosecutor has been sicced on a presidential administration, we've known what the allegations were. That's because what they were accused of doing was criminal. Yet, as the appearance of scandal engulfs this administration, we still don't know what crimes Trump and his subordinates are suspected of committing. Or even if they are suspected of committing crimes at all."

Which was all the more reason that Trump was in a rage, and why he continued his tweets and public comments dissing Jeff Sessions. Some White House aides, including Trump's son-in-law, Jared Kushner, pleaded with the president to cease his public attacks on Sessions. His tweets, they said, diverted attention from serious issues like health care and tax reform. What's more, the only thing Trump's attacks seemed to accomplish was to infuriate Sessions' Senate allies, of which there were many.

A tiny, unprepossessing Southerner with an ingratiating manner, Sessions was a rock-solid conservative. He had been the first establishment figure in the Republican Party to support Trump for president, and he had been a loyal advocate during the campaign. He had spent twenty years in the United States Senate, where, as the saying goes, he went along to get along, and where he was part of that chamber's old boys' club. The members of the club vowed that, if Trump fired Sessions as attorney general, they would refuse to confirm Trump's choice of a replacement.

With the exception of Joe Manchin of West Virginia, every Senate Democrat had voted against Sessions at his confirmation hearing. But in a spectacular display of hypocrisy, the Democrats suddenly rallied to Sessions' defense in order to embarrass the president.

The buzz around the Justice Department and the FBI was that Trump was so agitated by the ever-widening Russia probe that he would fire both Sessions and Special Counsel Robert Mueller, which was almost certain to ignite the biggest political firestorm since Nixon's Saturday Night Massacre.

However, under the strict interpretation of the law, the president himself couldn't fire Mueller. He had to order someone in the Justice Department to do that. If the president gave such an order, former CIA Director John Brennan urged that the Justice Department official refuse to obey it.

"I think it's the obligation of some executive branch officials to refuse to carry that out," said Brennan, who was essentially recommending an insurrection of the bureaucracy against the president.

Prosecutors and veteran FBI agents who had worked with the fiercely independent Mueller believed that he would never give an inch under pressure from the White House. Mueller, they said, would not be satisfied to limit his investigation to the question of Russian meddling in the presidential election and the allegation that the Trump campaign had colluded with the Russians.

"Bob will take the investigation all the way to its logical conclusion—way beyond the Russian collusion questions," said a former Justice Department prosecutor who worked as a consultant for the FBI. "You don't hire the kind of A Team that Mueller has assembled unless you believe you're going to get the goods. These guys are world-class experts in everything from campaign finance violations to money laundering.

"It's like giving a bunch of cops a search warrant for drugs," this source continued. "They'll tear your house apart—and not only for drugs. They'll search for weapons, stolen merchandise, cash, anything."

In an interview in the Oval Office with the *New York Times*, Trump warned that Mueller would cross a red line if he expanded his probe into the Trump family's business ties. Like all red lines, this was meant as a threat, and unlike Barack Obama's failure to back up his red line on Syrian chemical weapons, Trump was known to make good on his threats.

However, a day after the *Times* published Trump's red-line remark, Bloomberg ran a story that Mueller was investigating the purchase of a Trump mansion in Florida by a Russian oligarch, as well as other business transactions that Trump and his family had had with Russians.

With that leak to Bloomberg, the special counsel fired a shot across Trump's bow, and set up an epic clash that could end with Mueller's firing and a constitutional crisis.

■ ■ ■

"A slew of dismissals—ending with Mueller's firing—is not too hard to imagine," wrote Olivia Beavers in *The Hill*. "President Trump's critics argue that this would be the straw that breaks the camel's back. Impeachment would be inevitable.

"Don't bet on it," Beavers continued. "Impeachment is first and foremost a political process. House and Senate Republicans will have to decide to impeach their president. And even if the White House does act to prevent itself from being investigated, it's by no means clear that such a breach of norms would be sufficient to push congressional Republicans over the edge."

Despite Trump's rash and often outrageous behavior, congressional Republicans knew which way the wind was blowing in conservative circles, and it wasn't blowing against Trump. Commentators at *National Review*, most of whom were otherwise wobbly on Trump, supported his decision to fire Comey, as did influential talk-show hosts like Rush Limbaugh and Sean Hannity. Between 80 and 90 percent of Republicans had a favorable opinion of him (which was standard for most recent presidents), and attacks by Republican Never-Trumpers failed to resonate with his supporters, who voted for him in the first place because they felt under siege, financially and culturally, and who now rallied to Trump's cause because *he* was under siege.

"I love it when they bash him," a Wisconsin Republican told the *New York Times*, "because it tells me he's doing the right thing."

EPILOGUE

THE VIEW FROM TRUMP COUNTRY

For the past twenty years, the American presidency has faced a rolling crisis of legitimacy. Three of our recent presidents—Clinton, Bush, and Obama—have all been stigmatized as illegitimate by their critics. None of them, however, has had to face the day in, day out battering ram of resistance that has confronted Donald Trump.

What's made the attacks on Trump so different from those against his predecessors is that the assaults haven't come from just one direction—the opposition party. They've come from all directions, and all at once.

The Democrats have resisted everything that Trump supports.

The conservative intelligentsia and their allies in Congress have heaped scorn and contempt on the president.

And the media has run amok in their never-ending effort to run Trump out of office.

"The Court of Mad King Donald is not a presidency," Eugene Robinson, a *Washington Post* opinion writer, declared in a column that captured the unhinged mentality of the anti-Trump resistance. "It is an affliction, one that saps the life out of our democratic institutions, and it must be fiercely resisted if the nation as we know it is to survive."

Some of the people I interviewed for this book predicted that it was all over for Trump; they couldn't imagine how any president, even one as tough and battle-tested as Donald Trump, could possibly survive the kind of onslaught he's sustained from his critics.

Others said that many of Trump's problems were self-inflicted. These critics focused on his seemingly impulsive use of Twitter to lash out at his real or presumed enemies, and they quoted Richard Nixon's remark in his famous TV interview with David Frost: "I brought myself down. I gave them a sword, and they stuck it in and they twisted it with relish."

"When he's had enough," wrote Frank Rich in *New York* magazine, "I suspect he'll find a way to declare 'victory,' blame his departure on a conspiracy by America's (i.e., his) 'enemies,' and vow to fight another day on a network TBA. But as was also true with Nixon, some time and much patience will be required to wait for the endgame."

In my view, Trump's critics are indulging in wishful thinking. He isn't going anywhere. He's going to serve out his term in office. For despite the overwhelming hostility that he has faced since Day One, the view from Trump Country is far brighter than most people imagine.

His supporters ignore his clumsy mistakes and oafish tweets. They continue to have his back. Given a second chance, the vast majority of Republicans say they'd vote for him again.

More than two-thirds of the voters in counties that he won in 2016 endorse his willingness to take action if North Korea develops nuclear-tipped intercontinental ballistic missiles. A majority support his push for a ban on entry into the United States of refugees from high-risk Muslim-majority countries.

They even liked his politically incorrect remarks to law enforcement officers, when Trump urged them not to be "too nice" in dealing with the sadistic thugs of MS-13, an international criminal gang, often illegal aliens, who have been responsible for multiple murders in the United States.

"Like when you guys put somebody in the car and you're protecting their head, you know, the way you put their hand over" their head, he said, putting his own hand above his head. "I said, 'You can take the hand away, okay?'"

That brought a ton of criticism from official police organizations, civil rights groups, defense lawyers, and the media, but it brought laughter and cheers from his audience of policemen and women—and a silent nod of approval from his supporters across the country who are sick of hyper-violent gangs like MS-13, distressed by crimes committed by illegal aliens, and appalled at the Left's hostility to the police. Trump's base of white working class voters believe in law and order and, because of their economic circumstances, they are often on the frontline when crime goes unpunished. For a long time, they have felt that no one defended their interests. Trump does.

"During an era when wealthy white Americans have learned to sympathetically imagine the lives of the poor, people of color, and LGBTQ people," writes Joan C. Williams in her new book *White Working Class*, "the white working class has been insulted or ignored during precisely the period when their economic fortunes tanked."

"Mr. Trump's ability to appeal to these voters is the reason he won and the reason his base isn't abandoning him, with or without a significant legislative victory," adds Jason L. Riley in the *Wall Street Journal*.

While his enemies feast on stories of White House dysfunction and intrigue—including the resignations of Press Secretary Sean Spicer and the firings of Chief of Staff Reince Priebus and strategic adviser Steve Bannon—Trump has moved ahead on his campaign pledge to reinvigorate the American economy.

"Six months into his presidency, Donald Trump's detractors portray him as a do-nothing president with no big wins on issues such as health care, taxes and infrastructure," wrote the *Wall Street Journal's* Greg Ip in an article headlined "The Mythical Do-Nothing Presidency." "That may be true if the benchmark is legislation, but that is an incomplete benchmark. To gauge a president's impact, you have to go beyond the laws he signs to the vast authority he wields through departments and agencies that apply the law. On that score, Mr. Trump is on track to do a lot."

In the introduction to this book, I made a promise to my readers. I said that if you wanted to join the effort to prevent the villains from destroying our president and our democracy, this book would be your guide.

When the villains raise their shrill voices to denounce Trump, do not be faint of heart. Here is your answer—a dozen of Trump's top accomplishments in his first year in office:[1]

1. He nominated and successfully guided the confirmation of Neil Gorsuch as an associate justice of the Supreme Court, tipping the Court back in a conservative direction.
2. He assembled the finest Cabinet in recent memory.
3. He presided over the biggest increase in consumer confidence in sixteen years and a stock market that added $4 trillion in value.
4. He granted a permit to begin construction of the Keystone XL and Dakota Access pipelines, and reopened Alaska's National Petroleum Reserve to oil and gas exploration—major initiatives that would make America energy independent.
5. He withdrew America from the job-killing Paris Climate Accord and the Trans-Pacific Partnership.
6. He increased military spending by more than $70 billion.
7. He began rebuilding the foundations of America's strategic partnerships in the Muslim world, and repaired America's tattered relationship with Israel.
8. He asked for—and received—promises of increased financial support from members of the North Atlantic Treaty Organization.

9. He brought Mexico and Canada back to the negotiating table to rewrite the North American Free Trade Agreement so that it would be more favorable to American manufacturers.
10. He rolled back dozens of Environmental Protection Agency regulations that harmed business.
11. He reversed the Obama administration's Federal Communications Commission's decision to regulate Internet-service providers, and he sped up the Food and Drug Administration's approval of new drugs.
12. He started work on The Wall, and reduced by 70 percent the number of illegal immigrants attempting to enter the United States.

And that's just for starters.

So to the villains and all his other detractors, we have a message: Don't bet against Donald Trump!

APPENDIX A

THE BRITISH DOSSIER

CONFIDENTIAL/SENSITIVE SOURCE

COMPANY INTELLIGENCE REPORT 2016/080

US PRESIDENTIAL ELECTION REPUBLICAN CANDIDATE
DONALD TRUMP'S ACTIVITIES IN RUSSIA AND COMPROMISING
RELATIONSHIP WITH KREMLIN

Summary

Russian regime has been cultivating, supporting and assisting TRUMP for at least 5 years. Aim, endorsed by PUTIN, has been to encourage splits and divisions in western alliance.

So far TRUMP has declined various sweetener real estate business deals offered him in Russia in order to further the Kremlin's cultivation of him. However, he and his inner circle have accepted a regular flow of intelligence from the Kremlin, including on his Democratic and other political rivals.

Former top Russian intelligence officer claims FSB has compromised TRUMP through his activities in Moscow sufficiently to be able to blackmail him. According to several knowledgeable sources, his conduct in Moscow has included perverted sexual acts which have been arranged/monitored by the FSB.

However, there were other aspects to TRUMP'S engagement with the Russian authorities. One of which had borne fruit for them was to exploit TRUMP'S personal obsessions and sexual perversion in order to obtain suitable 'kompromat' (compromising material) on him. According to Source D, where s/he had been present, TRUMP'S (perverted) conduct in Moscow including hiring the presidential suite of the Ritz Carlton Hotel, where he knew President and Mrs. OBAMA (whom he hated) had stayed on one of their official trips to Russia, and defiling the bed where they had slept by employing a number of prostitutes to perform a 'golden showers' (urination) show in front of him. The hotel was known to be under FSB control with microphones and concealed cameras in all the main rooms to record anything they wanted.

COMPANY INTELLIGENCE REPORT 2016/0895

RUSSIA/US PRESIDENTIAL ELECTION: FURTHER INDICATIONS OF EXTENSIVE CONSPIRACY BETWEEN TRUMP'S CAMPAIGN TEAM AND THE KREMLIN

Summary

Further evidence of extensive conspiracy between TRUMP'S campaign team and Kremlin, sanctioned at highest levels and involving Russian diplomatic staff based in the US.

TRUMP associate admits Kremlin behind recent appearance of DNC e-mails on WikiLeaks as means of maintaining plausible deniability.

Agreed exchange of information established in both directions. TRUMP'S team using moles within DNC and hackers in the US as well as outside in Russia. PUTIN motivated by fear and hatred of Hillary CLINTON. Russians receiving intel from TRUMP'S team on Russian oligarchs and their families in the US.

Mechanism for transmitting this intelligence involves "pension" disbursements to Russian emigres living in US as cover, using consular officials in New York, DC and Miami.

Suggestion from source close to TRUMP and MANAFORT that Republican campaign team happy to have Russia as media bogeyman to mask more extensive corrupt business ties to China and other emerging countries.

COMPANY INTELLIGENCE REPORT 2016/94

RUSSIA: SECRET KREMLIN MEETINGS ATTENDED BY TRUMP ADVISOR CARTER PAGE IN MOSCOW (JULY 2016)
Summary

TRUMP advisor CARTER PAGE holds secret meetings in Moscow with [Igor] SECHIN and senior Kremlin Internal Affairs official, [Igor] DIVYEKIN.

SECHIN raises issues of future bilateral US-Russia energy co-operation and associated lifting of western sanctions against Russia over Ukraine. PAGE non-committal in response.

DIVEYKIN discusses release of Russian dossier of 'kompromat' on TRUMP's opponent, Hillary CLINTON, but also hints at Kremlin possession of such material on TRUMP.

COMPANY INTELLIGENCE REPORT 2016/136

RUSSIA/US PRESIDENTIAL ELECTION: FURTHER DETAILS OF TRUMP LAWYER COHEN'S SECRET LIAISON WITH THE KREMLIN

Summary

Kremlin insider reports TRUMP lawyer [Michael] COHEN's secret meeting/s with Kremlin officials in August 2016 was/were held in Prague.

Russian parastatal Rossotrudnichestvo used as cover for this liaison and promises in Czech capital may have been used for the meeting/s.

Pro-PUTIN leading Duma figure, [Konstantin] KOSA-CHEV, reportedly involved as 'plausible deniable' facilitator and may have participated in the August meeting/s with COHEN.

COMPANY INTELLIGENCE REPORT 2016/105

RUSSIA/UKRAINE: THE DEMISE OF TRUMP'S CAMPAIGN MANAGER PAUL MANAFORT

Summary

Ex-Ukrainian President [Viktor] YANUKOVYCH confides directly to PUTIN that he authorized kick-back payments to MANAFORT, as alleged in western media. Assures Russian President however there is no documentary evidence/trail.

AN FBI FIELD REPORT ON THE "RESISTANCE"

CONFIDENTIAL

Report to the Office of FBI Director from field offices Los Angeles, San Francisco, Detroit and New York

Limit Distribution [only director's office and field office heads]
Delivered May 29, 2017
Signed acceptance

Summary

Following over 2000 interviews in the field the consensus opinion is that the opposition is largely in California, and to a lesser degree in New York and Washington, D.C., but there are millions across the country who are willing to engage in activity publicly demonstrating their opposition to the Trump Administration.

The largest organizations are the Courage Campaign, who at one point claimed membership of slightly over a million. Most of these "members" actually only signed on for on-line membership, many have made small contributions. The group is scattered and consists mostly of small cell groups. There is no evidence this organization advocates violence, instead encouraging signing petitions and lobbying politicians.

Some can be described as militant but there was no open inclination to violent incitement.

It's Going Down

In the present political climate, the rhetoric is extremely overheated. Even the Sierra Club's leader Michael Brune has said, "We will fight like dogs in the street." The opinion of the agents is that the mainstream organizations pose no threat and should be allowed to carry out their constitutional rights to protest.

Of greater concern is the Berkeley based militant group It's Going Down, which has cells that communicate through the internet from colleges in all 50 states, as well as Canada and Mexico. This organization has accepted responsibility for the violence and destruction in Berkeley despite comments by Professor Robert Reich and UC Berkeley Police Chief Margo Bennett that the incidents were performed by "outside agitators." One of the arrestees in the incidents was identified as a student of Professor Reich.

This organization is under active investigation by the Bureau owing to their interstate funding nature and their inclination to physically attack banks and savings and loans with fire bombs, rocks and iron rods.

They raise funds through PayPal and Bitcoin.

It's Going Down has been active since late 2015, publishes magazines and videos encouraging violent demonstrations against banks and other institutions. They refer to their organization as anarchist and say they collect funds to finance "uprisings and rebellions." It bills itself as an "anarchist" group and claims ties to other violent anarchist groups abroad, including Peru.

ACTION REQUIRED

It is recommending that all intelligence the bureau gathers on this organization be shared with the Secret Service.

There are numerous off-shoot organizations of It's Going Down, including Final Straw, which advocates for the release of federal prisoners who have been convicted of sabotage, arson, bank robbery and bombing. At the top of the list, which has been widely disseminated on various web sites, are Joan Laman who was convicted of armed robbery and bank robbery in the 1980s and is serving a fifty-year term in federal prison. Another on recent posts is Marius Mason who is serving time for sabotage and arson.

There is no evidence that this group has done more than petition for the release of these federal prisoners. There is no evidence they have tried to organize a prison escape. But they are obviously encouraging violent activism by heralding their crimes.

Funding for this group includes small donations sent through bitcoin and PayPal. They use their funding to record podcasts and regular hour long radio broadcasts on community radio stations ranging from Asheville, NC to Fairbanks, AK.

Some funding also comes from George Soros, who they refer to in their fund raising broadcasts and literature as "Daddy Warbucks."

The organization and its subgroups advocate work outs for its members and training to engage in "street fighting." It is clear that their motives include preparing members, both male and female to engage in hand-to-hand combat with police and guards of banks and other financial institutions.

Several members of the group, arrested in the fire-bombing and sabotage in Berkeley described to local police and later FBI agents the nature of the training they received which included the making of Molotov cocktails and the use of tire irons, among other weaponized tools to do the most destruction possible and to use as weapons against law enforcement personnel who get in their way.

The training, which takes place often in public gyms that are sympathetic to the cause, particularly in the San Francisco Bay Area, is unprecedented in recent years. It is nearly on a par with ISIS training minus the suicide bombs.

The organization complains about the "liberal fetishization of non-violence," in its writing online, and claims "they are more interested in doing what is right, not what is legal."

Veteran agents compare the level of training in preparation for violent confrontation with law enforcement to the Black Panther training in the 1970's.

There is intelligence the group and/or off-shoots are planning a training camp in rural Massachusetts over the summer.

There have always been militant groups, particularly associated with UC Berkeley, but the agitprop against the current administration is unusually virulent, and potentially dangerous.

There have been intercepts recently that the organization is in contact with Muslim militants both in Detroit and overseas. There was a suggestion that they wish to liaise with some radical elements with the hope of learning more aggressive and violent tactics. This group has made common cause against Islamic Americans who have come out against any imposition of Sharia Law in the U.S., which intel suggests is a condition to get cooperation from extremists.

This is a concern that is actionable and must be closely monitored.

Government Sabotage

The Bureau has gotten actionable intelligence that there is, within the federal government, a growing and organized movement to block or interfere with administration policy decisions.

There have been regular organized meetings of large numbers of government workers at a church in the Columbia Heights area of the District where plans have been discussed to actively sabotage government programs they disagree with. These would include immigration enforcement, crackdowns on welfare fraud and any weakening of environmental rules. Plus, there is concern that some dissenting government workers might be dislodged from their positions by the Trump Administration.

There is evidence that, while there is a great deal of agitation within the government there are non-government individuals associated with unions and immigration and environmental groups who are behind these meetings.

Legal groups have been teaching some of these government employees what they can get away with doing in terms of delaying enforcement and what they cannot in terms of refusing to obey orders, which would constitute going on strike and get them dismissed under civil service rules.

One management level government employee said, "Bureaucrats are going to delay, drag their feet and throw roadblocks in the way of unconscionable actions by the Trump White House. It is going to become impossible to get these actions done."

There is a legal gray area here that the bureau has been very careful to avoid in terms of free speech and right to assemble. Legally government employees have the same rights as any other Americans to protest what the government is doing provided they do it on their own time.

Presently there is no sign of a revolt within the federal government.

But the situation is being monitored with a concern that this movement could lead to outright sabotage and interfere with the day-to-day functioning of the U.S. Government.

Cyber Security

A combination of intercepts and informants indicate that another way the movement people are planning to block the administration is through hacking or cyber-attacks on government data systems.

A San Francisco based group called The Sum of Us says "Donald Trump's agenda is an existential threat to our communities and democracy," and suggests that the administration is going to use Silicon Valley to create a registry of Muslims to deport.

Intelligence from informants and intercepts suggest that there are numerous individuals who may be creating plans to hack into and destroy any such registry.

This threat has been referred to the National Cyber Investigation Joint Task Force, which works with the entire Intelligence Community, and all 56 FBI field offices.

While there is currently no evidence that such a registry is planned or being created it is a concern for the Cyber Security division of the bureau and the possibility that such a plan to alter or destroy U.S. Government files is being investigated actively.

ACTION REQUIRED

APPENDIX C

AN FBI FIELD REPORT ON THE RADICAL "RESISTANCE"

REPORT TO OFFICE OF DIRECTOR FBI AND FIELD OFFICES

CONFIDENTIAL

Office of Director and Field Offices Informational Report
Delivered July 11, 2017

Summary

Task force covered G-20 meeting in Hamburg studied intel from local authorities, Interpol and other assets, determined that as assumed U.S. based anarchist/radical groups had traveled to Germany and took part in the violence. There is also evidence of meetings between these individuals and associates of ISIS. There is clearly overwhelming evidence that there are growing ties between U.S. radicals and the Islamic State as well as several offshoots and splinter group affiliates.

There is an urgent need to closely surveil the identified individuals.

ISIS

While there has been military progress in Iraq against the Islamic State, their influence in Europe and throughout the world is clearly growing. Now that the bureau has determined they have followers in the radical U.S. resistance movement in the United States, it is clear there will be additional violence in the attacks on law enforcement and U.S. institutions including banks.

Ties between three key leaders of the Oakland group [names redacted] met in Hamburg with a leader of the AQAP [Al Qaeda in the Arabian Peninsula] and the AQIM [Al Qaeda in the Islamic Maghreb]. The leader from AQAP is an Egyptian born male [name redacted] who is known to be in charge of finances and recruiting for the group.

There is evidence from informants that he is helping the Oakland group acquire the weapons they are seeking, primarily bomb making equipment and toxic chemicals and gasses.

One of the men from Oakland traveled to Syria to meet with ISIS, the purpose was for training in tactics, but was thought to be primarily a bonding visit to discuss possible massive disruptive attacks on the U.S.

While in Hamburg several of the Oakland based criminals were photographed throwing Molotov cocktails and wielding iron bars, which have been their weapons of choice, though they are almost certainly on the verge of upping the caliber of their weaponry for use in the U.S.

Despite having their faces covered by masks they were positively identified.

(**Action required**)

This group and their connections with the radical Islamic groups must be disrupted and destroyed.

Action has been taken with the appropriate agencies to see that these named individuals will be identified when they return to the United States. It has not been determined if they will be detained or surveilled.

There have been a number of clashes where members of radical movement have travelled to Syria or Iraq with the goal of meeting with ISIS or its affiliates and never returned. The intelligence is not that they joined the group and stayed, but that they were executed.

It appears to be one of the rare instances where the group does not crow about its summary executions but keeps quiet. Again the intel from informers is that they don't want the radicals—who are after all infidels—to be scared away.

Making some sort of common cause with Americans who are determined to commit violence against the U.S. makes them potentially very useful to radical Islam.

There is a body of evidence from chatter and informants that such a collaboration would not end well for the U.S. radicals. They would almost certainly be dispatched in the manner of the 9/11 hijackers, most not being aware until the end they were doomed.

It would not be in the Islamists best interests if the U.S. radicals who carried out a strike were captured and interrogated.

Numerous interviews have been carried out by associates of this group and have yielded some actionable intelligence, but the decision is to wait until the movement can be infiltrated and it is guaranteed that all criminal behavior can be identified and successfully prosecuted before any move is made.

Universities

Cooperation on this investigation with the University of California Berkeley has been less than agents would have liked. Obviously, it is a sensitive situation and has been handled with delicacy and strict adherence to bureau policy and the law.

It is clear that these individuals hide among the students and count on the fact that they will get protection from the academic community. They may not agree with the extreme violence that the radicals practice but they clearly agree with them on resistance to the current administration's perceived policies and goals.

The universities across the country where the radicals operate are extremely useful for their goals. They use the school's facilities to make posters to be distributed to resistance protesters. The college drama departments have been used in many cases to make masks and other disguises.

Electronic bulletin boards are used to quickly get word out to like-minded students about the dates and places of marches. These bulletin boards are often closed groups meaning that only students can access them.

When they are injured in violent confrontations with police, they can seek treatment at student health facilities with reasonable assurance the incident will not be reported to police the way a public or private hospital or clinic would likely do in the wake of violent street clashes.

Nature of the Organization

The nature of the organization we are dealing with is that it is not organized. Much like worldwide radical Islam, the so-called members are only united by a common ideology and a love of inflicting violence upon those perceived as the enemy. They all agree that chaos and violence against the government and business institutions—particularly banking—is a positive good.

It's not the kind of thing that needs to be written down or even much discussed.

There are no membership rolls, no rules and no hierarchy of leadership. The goal is simple and unstated: violent assaults with no warning or apparent reason. That is the nature of terror and the reason it is so terrifying.

The organization has no name, but it has hundreds of names. Often splinter groups on college campuses are formed into groups with innocuous names and benign purposes like the bird watchers, but most hide under pro environmental names.

The reason for organizing is that they apply for funding from the university, as well as the use of space to meet, hide their equipment and escape if they are on the run from law enforcement. We have information that there are numerous caches of weaponized tools and the ingredients to manufacture improvised explosive devices on college campuses across the country.

This is the greatest challenge to law enforcement since the Weather Underground and the Black Panther Party.

Universities have a rather unique status as sanctuaries for undocumented aliens and even criminal anarchists.

The hardest thing to predict is: When will the next assault occur?

The past few months have been relatively very quiet. The chatter has been minimal. The best information is that there will be a major spike in violent activity when school is back in session in late August.

Prologue

1. After the 2012 assault on the U.S. consulate in Benghazi, Rice appeared on five Sunday TV shows and said that the attack had been motivated by an anti-Islamic video, when she knew that it had been a carefully planned strike carried out by a terrorist group associated with al-Qaeda. In 2014, after Obama exchanged five Taliban terrorists for Army Sergeant Bowe Bergdahl, who deserted his post in Afghanistan and put his fellow soldiers' lives at risk, Rice said Bergdahl had served with "honor and distinction."

Chapter 4

1. After retiring as a judge on the Georgia Court of Appeals, Yates' father, Kelley Quillian, committed suicide. "Certainly, losing any family member to suicide carries with it a special kind of pain," Yates said. "The manner in which he died was heartbreaking. None

of us ever really know what demons someone is carrying around or what is going through their head when opportunity and despair come together."

Chapter 5

1.   As attorney general, Lynch was not supposed to discuss ongoing cases with anyone in the White House, including the president and his advisers. She violated that restriction and kept Jarrett informed on an almost daily basis.

2.   Comey's decision to announce his findings without Justice Department involvement was based, at least in part, on an intelligence document claiming that Lynch had secretly assured the Clinton campaign that it had nothing to worry about regarding the email investigation. Comey was concerned that if the document became public, it would undermine the integrity of the FBI investigation. It turned out that the document was a fake—a fabrication by the Russian intelligence services.

Chapter 6

1.   Though Trump started tweeting in 2009, he also had access to Page Six of the *New York Post*. His leaks to the *Post* resulted in some classic tabloid headlines, including "Best Sex I've Ever Had."

Chapter 7

1.   Credit for assembling these quotations belongs to *Politico* magazine, which ran a story on November 5, 2016, titled "The 155 Craziest Things Trump Said This Election."

Chapter 8

1.   Spayd was wildly unpopular among the *Times'* reporters and editors for her critical columns of the paper's coverage. She was summarily fired by Arthur Sulzberger Jr., the *Times'* publisher, before she had finished the first year of her two-year contract.

Chapter 13

1.   I had several conversations with Trump in which he sounded less than optimistic about his chances.

Chapter 14

1.   On the eve of the 2016 presidential campaign, John Judis had second thoughts about the headlock the Democrats thought they had on the white working class. "It now appears that, in some form, the Republican era which began in 1980 is still with us," Judis conceded.

2.   MoveOn.org was formed in 1998 in opposition to the impeachment of President Bill Clinton. It got its name from its motto: "Time to move on."

3.   The alt-right is an ill-defined, loosely organized movement of America-first conservatives who oppose multiculturalism and political correctness.

Chapter 16

1.   The DA "Partners," who pay yearly dues ranging from $35,000 to $70,000 a year and are encouraged to contribute at least $200,000 a year to the organization, include Donald Sussman, Tom Steyer, Norman Lear, and George Soros' sons Jonathan and Alex.

Chapter 17

1.   There are 633 cities and counties that refuse to cooperate with the U.S. Immigration and Customs Enforcement Service.

2.   The ACLU received more than 350 online donations totaling almost $25 million in the days following Trump's election victory.

Chapter 18

1.   Rogers' trip raised the hackles of the Obama administration, which considered firing him. As things turned out, Rogers did not get the

top intelligence post but remained as director of the NSA under Trump.

2. According to James Comey, the soon-to-be-fired FBI director, many of those stories were "nonsense."

3. Michelle Obama had at least one reason to feel what hope felt like; she accepted an offer of a $20 million advance against royalties for her memoirs.

4. To start relations with the incoming Trump administration on a strong footing, Putin did not retaliate by expelling American diplomats from Russia.

Chapter 19

1. An abridged version of the dossier can be found in Appendix A.

2. Bernstein's collaborator in the Watergate story, Bob Woodward, was more fastidious; he said that there wasn't enough evidence of collusion between the Trump camp and the Russians to warrant the appointment of a special prosecutor.

3. "But that didn't stop [Obama's CIA chief James] Brennan from attaching [the document's] contents to the official report [he offered] the president," wrote Paul Sperry, a political commentator and frequent contributor to the *New York Post*. "He also included the unverified allegations in the briefing he gave Hill Democrats. In so doing, Brennan virtually guaranteed that it would be leaked, which it promptly was. In short, Brennan politicized raw intelligence. In fact, he politicized the entire CIA. Langley vets say Brennan was the most politicized director in the agency's history."

Chapter 20

1. Trump painted a bleak picture of "American carnage"—abandoned factories, an economy in decline, communities under siege by crime, gangs, and drugs—but he also promised a future of American renewal. The fact that Hillary Clinton, and apparently the Bushes, thought it was "disturbing" only underlined how distant and

unaware they were of the issues that drove Trump's supporters. Hillary's husband Bill was much better at feeling people's "pain."

2. The description of the inaugural day protests is drawn from a January 21, 2017, *Wall Street Journal* article written by Ben Kesling, Byron Tau, and Joseph De Avila.

Chapter 21

1. The stay was upheld by several federal appeals courts and ultimately wound up on the docket of the Supreme Court, which lifted the stay and allowed a limited travel ban.

Chapter 22

1. The Goldwater Rule was adopted after *Fact* magazine published an article stating that 1,189 of the 2,417 psychiatrists whom it polled deemed Barry Goldwater, the Republican presidential nominee in 1964, mentally unfit to be president of the United States. Goldwater later sued and won the libel case against the magazine.

Chapter 23

1. *"The Washington Post*, which has long hated Republicans, and Trump in particular, is leading the charge," noted the *Breitbart News* Network. "On February 15, seven of the eight stories on its online home page were anti-Flynn, anti-Trump—and, of course, pro-mainstream media."

2. Obama's CIA Director John Brennan, a man who had once voted for the Communist Party USA candidate for president, and whose dislike of Trump was plain and public, called Trump's tweeted remarks "outrageous."

3. For a complete version of the FBI field report see Appendix B.

4. The rule was not as "obscure" as Homans would have had his readers believe. Warren was censured for breaching Rule 19 of the Senate, which says that senators are not allowed to "directly or indirectly, by any form of words impute to another Senator or

to other Senators any conduct or motive unworthy or unbecoming a Senator."

5. When Charles Murray, the libertarian political scientist (and, ironically, Never-Trumper), attempted to deliver a speech at Middlebury College, he was shouted down by students and outside agitators. Murray attempted to move his speech to another location, but he and a Middlebury professor were attacked by violent demonstrators. The professor was sent to the hospital with a neck injury and a concussion. Three thousand miles away from Middlebury, Vermont, Evergreen State College in Olympia, Washington, had to hold its commencement thirty miles from campus because anarchists demanded "a day of absence" for white students.

6. While Scalise was in the hospital recovering from multiple surgeries, MSNBC's Joy Ann Reid went on a tweet storm attacking him for his views on same-sex marriage, gun control, health care, and other issues.

7. See Appendix C.

Chapter 24

1. RootsAction boasted that it was endorsed by a veritable who's who of progressives, including political activists Barbara Ehrenreich, Cornel West, Daniel Ellsberg, Glenn Greenwald, Naomi Klein, and Phil Donahue.

2. Among those who belonged to the "demented" wing were *New York Times* columnist Charles M. Blow, an avowed Trump hater, who admitted he was seized by "a throbbing anxiety" every time he thought about impeaching the president; and Democratic Congressman Mark Pocan of Wisconsin, who compared the countdown to Trump's impeachment to the "doomsday clock," a cold war symbol that represented the likelihood of global thermonuclear war.

3. Chelsea Manning's sentence was commuted by President Obama.

4.   After serving as a University of Montana law professor for twenty-three years, Natelson, an outspoken conservative, requested professor emeritus status. The law school faculty voted to deny him that status.

Chapter 26

1.   In addition to the Kalorama mansion, the former president, first lady, and Jarrett each have a government paid-for office.

Chapter 27

1.   "Yates, an Obama administration holdover, had a political agenda," reported the *New York Times*. "She was fired days later over her refusal to defend in court Mr. Trump's ban on travel for people from several predominantly Muslim countries."

Chapter 28

1.   Obama was away from home a great deal of time. In addition to trips to Hawaii and French Polynesia, he visited Italy, Germany, and Indonesia.
2.   In an exception to his stay-mum stance, Obama criticized Trump's decision to end DACA, the immigration program designed to protect illegal immigrants who were brought to the U.S. as children. He called Trump's decision "cruel" and "self-defeating."

Chapter 32

1.   Mueller wasted no time hiring a large staff, including several prosecutors who had donated money to the Clinton presidential campaign.

Chapter 34

1.   The university staff was so afraid of the violence that it installed an "escape hatch" in the chancellor's office.
2.   See Appendix C, "An FBI Field Report on the Radical 'Resistance.'"

3.   The Weather Underground, or the Weathermen, as the radical group was known colloquially, conducted a campaign of indiscriminate bombings in the 1970s. The Black Panther Party, a 1960s Marxist revolutionary group that called for the arming of African-Americans against the police, has been revived under new leadership in recent years.

Chapter 37

1.   Andrew Therriault, the former director of data science for the DNC, called Hillary's claims "fucking bullshit."

Chapter 38

1.   Obama had been a senator for four years before he was elected president.

Epilogue

1.   For several of the items on this list of Trump's successes, the author owes a debt of gratitude to Greg Ip and Kimberley A. Strassel of the *Wall Street Journal*.

INDEX